1989

CASE STUDIES IN HEALTH ADMINISTRATION
VOLUME SEVEN

ALTERNATIVE DELIVERY SYSTEMS

Approaches for the Health Care Executive

Samuel Levey, Ph.D.

and

James Hill, Ph.D.

Editors

Copyright 1988

Foundation of the

American College of Healthcare Executives

Chicago, Illinois

Library of Congress Cataloging-in-Publication Data

Alternative Delivery Systems.

    (Case studies in health administration; v. 7)
    "The selected case reports were submitted to the College in partial fulfillment of requirements for conferral of the status of Fellow" — Foreword
    Bibliography: p.
    1. Medical care — United States. 2. Health maintenance organizations — United States. 3. Ambulatory medical care — United States. 4. Home care services — United States. I. Levey, Samuel. II. Hill, James Norman. III. Series. [DNLM: 1. Ambulatory Care Facilities — United States. 2. Delivery of Health Care — trends — United States. 3. Health Maintenance Organizations — United States. 4. Insurance, Health — United States. W1 CA901PH v.7 / W 275 AA1 A392]
RA395.A3A48 1988   362.1   88–16298
ISBN 0–910701–40–7

Foundation of the American College
   of Healthcare Executives
840 N. Lakeshore Drive
Chicago, Illinois 60611
(312) 943–0544

Table of Contents

Part Two: Cases

AMERICAN COLLEGE OF HEALTHCARE EXECUTIVES

BOARD OF GOVERNORS

OFFICERS

1987-1988

CHAIRMAN

Francis J. Cronin, FACHE
President/CEO
Health NorthEast and Elliot Hospital
Manchester, New Hampshire

CHAIRMAN-ELECT

David H. Jeppson, FACHE
Executive Vice-President
Intermountain Health Care, Inc.
Salt Lake City, Utah

IMMEDIATE PAST-CHAIRMAN

D. Kirk Oglesby, Jr. , FACHE
President
Anderson Memorial Hospital
Anderson, South Carolina

PRESIDENT

Stuart A. Wesbury, Jr., Ph.D, FACHE
President
American College of Healthcare Executives
Chicago, Illinois

Foreword

Alternative delivery systems are no longer accessory means of health care financing and delivery, but instead now constitute an important sector of our health care system. The testimony of a marketplace increasingly crowded with HMOs, PPOs, and freestanding ambulatory care units is sufficient to convince traditionalists of this fact, and to corroborate the instincts of those critics who for years have urged the introduction of competitive plans and services as a means to contain rising health care costs.

An accessible overview of this subject that also offers practical guidance in the form of case reports is likely to benefit the health care executive. Many are familiar with the wide spectrum of alternative delivery systems; their knowledge has been acquired in disparate parts over the last several years. **Alternative Delivery Systems: Approaches for the Health Care Executive** presents a perspective on a health care system in intense transition and the alternative delivery system it has generated. It describes the current environment and speculates on the future. It also considers our social responsibilities in a market-driven health care industry. Finally, this volume offers a generalized approach to diversification, which serves as a frame of reference for commentaries on the cases.

Alternative Delivery Systems is the seventh in the series, Case Studies in Health Administration, published by the American College of Healthcare Executives. It has been edited by Samuel Levey, Hartman Professor and Head, Graduate Program in Hospital and Health Administration and Center for Health Services Research, at the University of Iowa, and James Hill, research associate. The selected case reports were submitted to the College in partial fulfillment of requirements for conferral of the status of Fellow.

Francis J. Cronin, FACHE
Chairman, Board of Governors
American College of
Healthcare Executives

Other volumes in the series:

Case Studies: Health Administration Volume Six:
Hospital Labor Relations. James O. Hepner (Editor). 1987.

Case Studies in Health Administration Volume Five: An
Economic Approach to Rationing Health Care Resources. Lanis
L. Hicks and Keith E. Boles (Editors). 1985.

Case Studies in Health Administration Volume Four: Ethics for Health Services Managers. Kurt Darr (Editor). 1985.

Case Studies in Health Administration Volume Three: Strategic Planning for Hospitals. Phillip N. Reeves (Editor). 1983.

Case Studies in Health Administration Volume Two: Hospital Administrator-Physician Relationships. James O. Hepner (Editor). 1980.

Case Studies in Health Administration Volume One: Health Planning for Emerging Multihospital Systems. James O. Hepner (Editor). 1978.

Any case study that manages to be at once unique and representative, illuminating the general experience as it describes the individual one, merits some regard. The reports in this volume possess this dual quality. They describe the particular events of a specific organizational history, yet concentrate on the elemental parts in addressing those questions that are asked by health managers as they create, acquire, or co-sponsor alternative delivery systems. The issues discussed in the following pages should be of interest to health care executives who are contemplating the introduction of new plans and services, and those concerned with the organization, financing, and marketing of such systems. This volume should also be useful to students and faculty in health management and related programs.

"Alternative delivery systems" (ADS) refers to an array of plans and services that have evolved into a vital segment of the United States health care system; it includes alternatives to traditional financing systems as well as inpatient services. In recent years, under the pressures of cost containment and shrinking inpatient admissions, providers have pursued opportunities in alternative delivery systems as a strategy for holding and enhancing their shares of the market. Purchasers of health care are similarly interested in plans and services that promise quality care at discount rates. For both provider and purchaser, the overriding incentive is the bottom line of economics: reductions in price, preferably without compromising the quality of services.

In each case report in this volume, a health care manager who has been involved with an alternative delivery system describes the circumstances that generated the plan, the implementation of the plan, and the results. Obviously, one key value to the reader of these first-hand accounts lies in the 20-20 hindsight afforded the author by the experience: since experimentation with diversification is often fraught with the difficulties of any untried enterprise, the documented processes and outcomes of cases, and the considered advice of colleagues will, we think, serve as important instruction. The purpose of this monograph--indeed, any casebook--is to offer guidance by way of example. It does so on the premise that a careful reconstruction of recent experience can provide a bridge between theory and practice.

This casebook presents a range of cases that introduce and discuss issues critical to success in ADS ventures. The categories that have been selected--HMOs, PPOs, and alternatives to inpatient care--are by no means a complete taxonomy, but merely the set of most prominent species. The cases have been selected on the basis of a combination of criteria: significance of the problem, exercise of management functions in addressing the problem, and creative thinking in problem solving. The material is presented in four parts: an overview of the major types of alternative delivery systems followed by three sets of cases. A commentary precedes each set, identifying and explaining the distinguishing elements of each case.

We would like to thank the College Fellows who permitted us to use their case reports in this volume:

Gary J. Blan   James W. Connolly
Kent A. Keahey   Richard L. McClarney
Marcus Merz   Mark A. Mrozek
James H. Mullins   Larry M. Narum
Peter K. Read   Larry S. Sanders
Gregory C. Van Pelt

We would also like to thank Peter A. Weil, the College's Director of Research and Public Policy, for his patience and understanding while awaiting the drafts of this casebook.

S. L., J. H.

Part One: Introduction

Health care managers who began their careers in the halcyon 1950s and 1960s confronted environments that are almost unrecognizable today. Financial pressures were largely unknown; strategic planning was invariably translated into decisions to expand facilities and services; matters of equity, quality, and access were in the forefront. Not surprisingly, after two decades the latter issues remain at the fore. Cost containment has joined them, however, generating enormous change in traditional models for the organization, financing, and delivery of health care. One feature of this change is the large-scale emergence of alternative delivery systems.

I. Background

1) Transition in the Health Care Industry

Health care is in a period of dramatic adjustment. Following the implementation of Medicare, stability in the organization, financing, and delivery of health care was disrupted by a crisis in costs, and the system-wide restructuring that followed has continued to this day, gaining momentum from President Reagan's decision to leave the shaping of the health care system to the free market. A prominent sign of this change is the rapid proliferation of HMOs, PPOs, outpatient substitutes for inpatient service (e.g., home health care, minor emergency centers), and "expanded mission" services such as wellness, fitness, childcare, long-term care, and retirement centers.

The precipitous rise in health care expenditures has given the issue of cost containment a much higher profile than ever before in the forum of public debate. Medicare and Medicaid, the aging of the population, the expansion of health insurance, the growth in the supply of health professionals, the explosion of medical technology, and sustained inflation in health care costs have pushed total outlays for health care to 11 percent of our gross national product, nearly $500 billion in 1987.

This upward curve of spending has been followed by a similar upturn in cost consciousness among purchasers. Incentives to manage health care costs that began tentatively as piecemeal efforts have now acquired a priority status among health care buyers (particularly business and government) as well as among many providers, and have generated the formulation and implementation of containment mechanisms such as prospective payment systems, and increased deductibles and co-payments.

Such cost-limiting initiatives have, of course, created new pressures for all health care providers. For hospitals, they have meant reimbursement caps, a declining inpatient census, and overcapacity. Between 1980 and 1985, annual admissions dropped from 166.5 to 144.6 per 1000 population, and the average length of stay fell from 7.2 to 6.5 days. [1] For new physicians, the mounting risks of establishing a solo practice have turned many to safer opportunities in alternative delivery systems, notably to salaried corporate medicine. In view of the prospects for still tighter controls on health care spending, the impact of a leveling of demand for health care and a growing surplus of physicians poses interesting questions regarding patterns of care in the years to come.

2) Responses of the Health Care Industry

Both purchasers and providers have taken active roles in revising the terms of health care delivery. With increasing competition for the health industry dollar, both have become players in the game of market-driven medical care. Health care purchasers, for their part, are beginning to recognize the unfolding buyers' market for health care services, and are now more inclined to comparison shop for cost-effective plans and services.

In their attempts to maintain current volume and attract new patients, providers have undertaken strategic adaptation ventures that have served to restructure the way health care is financed and delivered in this country. The health care network that has emerged as a result of this restructuring is illustrated in Figure 1.

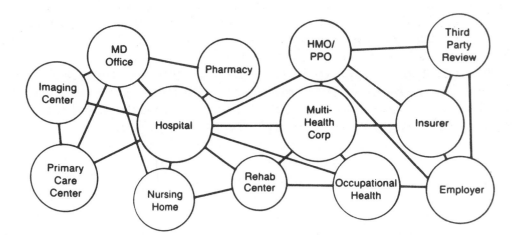

Figure 1. The health care network. (Russel C. Coile Jr.; The New Hospital, p.11. Rockville, MD: Aspen Publishers Inc., 1986. Reprinted with permission of the publisher.)

Many providers have become involved in "managed care," the popular term for an arrangement under which financial risk is assumed by the provider rather than a third party payor, and limits are imposed on utilization of services. Some providers offer consumers comprehensive care for established membership fees, and others offer discount rates for services. For sponsors of such alternatives, plans may be approached in various ways: development from the ground up, purchase of an existing service, or creation of a joint venture arrangement.

Among the provider's primary benefits in pursuing an alternative delivery system are maintenance and expansion of market share, effective competition with other providers, reduction of costs, enhancement of image as an innovator, and extension of social responsibility. In view of risks such as loss of capital and time, however, the risk-taker does well to analyze strategies, market potential, and financial effects. If, for example, a hospital-sponsored alternative delivery system is unable to offer services to a sufficiently large market, it risks financial hardship and collapse of the venture; by taking advantage of a network, however, it may achieve a larger degree of marketability.

As for ownership structure, an ADS enterprise may be either a solo operation or a joint venture. Solo offers the advantage of complete control of management and profits, while joint venturing provides enhanced access to investment capital and the distribution of risk between partners-- usually physicians and hospitals. Other benefits of joint venturing are the strengthening of the referral network of physicians and hospital, and the diversification of the hospital's revenue base.

The last five years in particular have witnessed a ferment of ADS activity on the part of health care organizations, physicians, and insurers. Between 1982 and 1986, the number of HMOs grew from 265 to 626 (shown in Figure 2), and enrollments climbed from 10.5 to 25.8 million. [2] During the same period, the number of PPOs grew from 40 to 454, and the number of individuals with the enrollment option rose to 10 percent of the U.S. population (Figure 3). [3] An indication of the surge in alternatives to inpatient care is provided by the rise in the number of free-standing surgicenters, up from 20 in 1982, to 690 in 1986. [4]

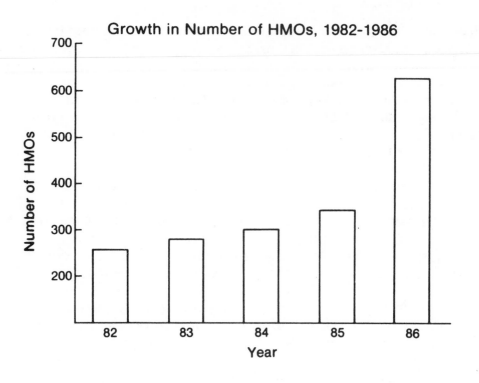

Fig. 2

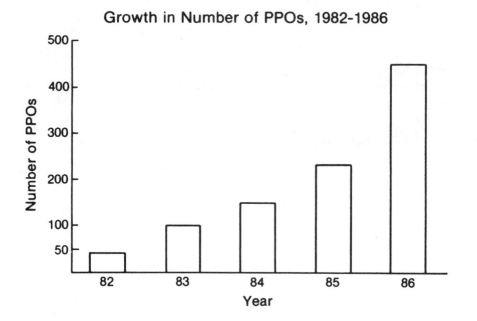

Fig. 3

A number of observers of the health care industry have applauded the dramatic growth, arguing that alternative delivery systems can significantly reduce the average patient's annual medical bill by a double-digit percentage as compared with conventional indemnity coverage. Other observers, unconvinced by available studies, maintain a detached neutrality, acknowledging the conditions that encourage a business orientation, without applauding them. Part of this caution may stem from responses on the part of entrepreneurs that go beyond HMOs, PPOs, and satellite clinics, to profit-making subsidiaries that are marginally health-related.

This brisk expansion of alternative delivery systems has been characterized as just one sign of an emergent "corporate ethos." Respected observers of this trend urge health care professionals to resist the excesses of this entrepreneurial spirit, on the rationale that medicine is first a profession and only secondarily a business. Necessity, they would argue, rather than the ability to sell new plans and products should determine their existence in the marketplace.

II. Alternative Delivery Systems

Although opinion converges on the broad meaning of "alternative delivery system," it divides on the issue of boundaries. What, for example, are the lines of demarcation between traditional and alternative? Evidence suggests that "alternative" may be something of a misnomer, since, as Ellwood notes, such delivery systems are fast becoming mainstream (i.e., traditional) means for buying and selling medical care. [5]

Does the phrase refer only to alternatives to fee-for-service third-party financing systems, such as the managed care plans, or is it a broad generic term that also includes all non-traditional health care services and programs that either replace inpatient care or extend the health care "mission" (e.g., home health care, wellness centers)? According to Goldsmith, a distinction exists: in his view, alternative delivery systems are just one of three new forces in the health care industry; the others are ambulatory care and "aftercare."[6] Under this scheme, ADS refers to full-service health plans, such as HMOs, PPOs, CMPs (competitive medical plans), IPOs (insured product options), and PCNs (primary care networks); ambulatory care refers to services such as outpatient surgery centers; aftercare is the term for home health care, hospice services, and geriatric outpatient care.

From our vantage point, all three developments qualify as ADS, since each offers a substitute plan or service for indemnity coverage or inpatient care. Consequently, we have drawn together under one heading the three groups mentioned above, and have concentrated on cases in three dominant categories: (1) HMOs and (2) PPOs, the two most popular alternatives to traditional indemnity health care benefit programs, and (3) assorted diversification activities.

1) Health Maintenance Organizations (HMOs)

A health maintenance organization is a health care plan that provides comprehensive medical services (i.e., inpatient, ambulatory, emergency, and preventive) to voluntarily enrolled members for a fixed premium. Under this arrangement, sponsors enroll subscribers and then operate within a budget to provide all necessary care. The economic viability of the HMO is dependent on the level of enrollment, as well as the maintenance of members' health, and restraint in the use of medical services.

Three HMO models currently dominate the marketplace: (1) staff, in which physicians are employed by the HMO in a centralized facility and are provided office space and administrative support; (2) group, in which the HMO contracts with a multispecialty medical group practice; and (3) independent practice associations (IPAs), alliances made up of individual physicians practicing out of their own offices (see Figure 4). In 1987, IPAs constituted the largest number of HMO plans, with 62 percent of the total; staff, group, and various configurations of less importance made up the balance. [7]

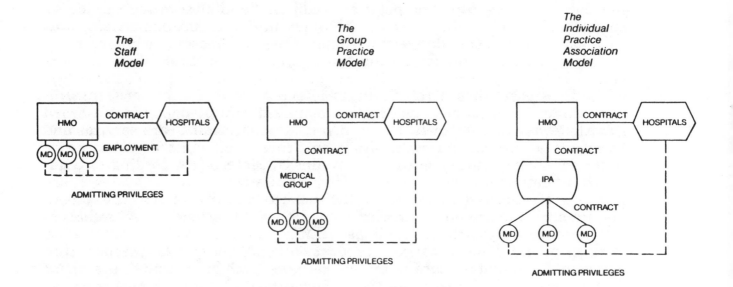

Figure 4. HMO models. (Norbert Goldfield and Seth Goldsmith, eds., Alternative Delivery Systems, p. 133. Rockville, MD: Aspen Publishers Inc., 1987. Reprinted with permission of the publisher.)

Distinguishing characteristics of the generic HMO include (1) a defined population of enrolled members; (2) voluntary enrollment by each member or family; (3) payments by the members, determined in advance for a specific period of time and made periodically; (4) medical services provided on a direct service basis rather than on an indemnity basis, and services provided to patients by HMO physicians for essentially all medical needs, with referrals to outside physicians controlled by HMO physicians. [8]

Among the chief selling points for HMOs are reduced health care costs, a comprehensive range of services, preventive programs (e.g., periodic checkups, inoculations), and an emphasis on convenient outpatient care. Disadvantages of the HMO arrangement include the absence of free choice for members in the selection of physician, bias in admission of members (i.e., younger, healthier individuals), and limited accessibility. (Although many HMOs do arrange for treatment of enrollees outside the HMO service area, some do not.)

Of the various species of alternative delivery systems currently in operation, HMOs have the longest history. While the origin of the phrase, "health maintenance organization" is as recent as 1970, the concept of comprehensive prepaid care for enrolled members through a designated provider can be traced to the "club" medicine of the nineteenth century under which industrial employers (e.g., mining, railroads) provided coverage to employees. Union-sponsored plans followed in this century, and in 1929 the Ross-Loos Health Plan, a provider-sponsored model, was introduced in Los Angeles. The well-known Kaiser plan was developed by Kaiser Industries for its employees in the 1930s, and it has grown steadily to become the major network in the HMO industry, with nearly five million enrollees in twelve states. Although conceived on a not-for-profit basis, HMOs are now dominated by for-profit plans; as of June 1987, investor-owned HMOs outnumbered not-for-profits 389 to 237. [9] Among the investor-owned are giant multi-market HMOs such as Maxicare Health Plans, United Healthcare Corporation, and Metlife Healthcare Management Corporation--all with multi-state service and enrollments in six or seven figures.

In the early 1970s, a national health strategy that emphasized the development of health maintenance organizations as a cost-saving alternative to conventional plans was introduced at the federal level. The passage of the Health Maintenance Act in 1973, in effect, launched this cost-saving strategy by generating federal funds for HMO operating grants and loans; in addition, it set the standards for a federally recognized HMO, and required that employers offer employees the option of joining an HMO. Further expanding the HMO market was the passage of the Tax Equity and Fiscal Responsibility Act in 1982, which enabled Medicare and Medicaid beneficiaries to enroll in HMOs.

2) Preferred Provider Organizations (PPOs)

Preferred provider organizations (PPOs) have been called a compromise between HMOs and traditional care--a middle ground between the HMO's prepaid care and closed circle of providers and the indemnity plan's fee-for-service treatment and principle of laissez-faire in the selection of provider. Its roots, similar to HMOs', can be traced to the nineteenth century and the low-cost service made available to industrial employees from a panel of providers hired by employers.

"Preferred provider organization" refers to a tripartite arrangement under which a sponsor negotiates with health care providers for discount services on behalf of enrollees. In more specific terms, it applies to a set of contracts between parties that offers prospectively negotiated fee-for-service care to subscribers from a panel of "preferred" providers. The latter may be physicians, hospitals, nursing homes, pharmacies, and home health providers (see Figure 5).

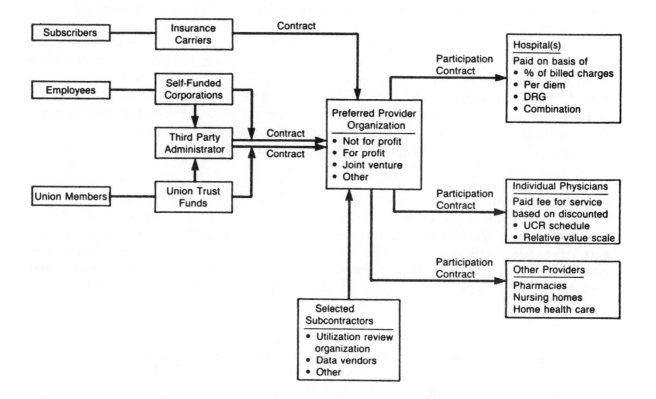

Figure 5. Preferred Provider Organization. (S. Brian Barger, et al., The PPO Handbook, p. 5. Rockville, MD: Aspen Publishers Inc., 1984. Reprinted with permission of the publisher.)

Although most plans encourage enrollees to use a designated panel of providers, some plans permit the use of non-PPO physicians, with the proviso that the enrollee will pay the difference in rates. (In contrast to this arrangement, an HMO would require the "maverick" enrollee to pay the full fee.)

Key selling points of PPOs include discounted rates for services and, for providers, a higher volume of patients. Further, providers are able to enlarge their pool of patients without incurring the financial risks of HMOs. Drawbacks of PPO arrangements include the possibility of greater provider utilization, difficulty of selecting cost-efficient providers, and cost-shifting to non-PPO patients by providers.

Among the critical external variables that determine the success or failure of a PPO are the demographic make-up of the population, business coalition activity, the existence of competition (particularly HMOs), physician manpower, and low hospital occupancies. Internal variables include benefits package, discount rates on services, provider reimbursement system, and the effectiveness of the utilization review process.

The tremendous diversity among PPOs has led one observer to remark, "If you've seen one PPO, you've seen one PPO. " Although a range of variations exists, the three most common types of PPOs are (1) open, in which the subscriber is given freedom to choose a provider; (2) lock-in, in which the subscriber makes a periodic choice of either providers designated by the PPO, or those outside the system; and (3) exclusive provider, in which only one option is offered to subscribers.

Five key components of preferred provider organizations are (1) a limited number of provider hospitals and physicians; (2) negotiated fee schedules; (3) utilization review; (4) incentives for consumers to use providers; and (5) prompt provider claim settlement. The four most frequently found types of PPO sponsors are (1) entrepreneurs; (2) employers; (3) insurers; and (4) providers. Insurance carriers and providers make up the largest number of sponsors, and the balance is divided between investors and self-insured employers.

3) Alternatives to Inpatient Care: Diversification Activities

Faced with a reduced demand for acute care services and a reimbursement system that rewards the expeditious discharge of patients, hospitals have embraced diversification options as a defensive strategy. Competition for patients has produced a wide range of new products and services, one measure of which is the proliferation of hospital-sponsored programs. According to the 1987 Environmental Assessment of the American Hospital Association, *Between 1981 and 1985, the number of community hospital-based outpatient departments rose 27 percent, alcoholism and chemical dependency programs increased*

30   percent, outpatient rehabilitation programs were up 17 percent and outpatient psychiatric programs 11 percent. In addition, hospitals are becoming more involved in sponsoring freestanding ambulatory care centers. [10] Three of the fastest rising diversification options are outpatient surgical care, home health care, and specialty services; one indication of their growth is the history of their progress in community hospital diversification activities between 1981 and 1985, as shown in Figure 5.

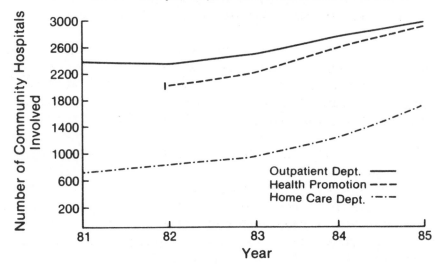

Figure 5. AHA Environmental Assessment Overview 1987. Reprinted with permission of the publisher.

The three primary settings for ambulatory surgery are (1) the in-hospital facility, (2) the freestanding hospital-affiliated facility, and (3) the freestanding independent facility. Between 1980 and 1985, in-hospital outpatient surgical procedures increased more than 100 percent. [11] The volume of hospital outpatient surgery rose from 2.6 million procedures in 1979 to 6.9 million in 1985. [12] In 1986, freestanding centers performed over one million surgical operations: of that number, hospital-operated centers (9.4 % of the total) conducted 11.8 percent; chain-operated centers (18.1%) accounted for 25.5 percent of the surgeries, and independent facilities (72.5%) performed 62.7 percent of the procedures. It is predicted that by the end of the decade, more than 800 freestanding outpatient surgery centers will be in operation, up from 592 in 1986. [13]

Another fast-growing alternative to traditional inpatient treatment is home health care. Outpatient care in the patient's home offers the advantages of comfort and a familiar living environment, as well as a significant cost saving over inpatient hospital care. The broad field of home health care can be broken down into four basic services: (1) Medicare-certified home health agencies; (2) private home care services; (3) high technology home therapy; and (4) durable medical equipment.

Competition among sponsors in the home health care field is intensifying: new programs are being introduced at a rapid rate, and sponsors already in the home care business are attempting to expand their scope of services and geographical coverage. Among those agencies showing the strongest growth rates are hospital-based, proprietary, and private non-profit. Among the factors accounting for this expansion are the aging of the population, the increase in portable technology, and growing consumer acceptance of home care as a desirable alternative to inpatient care. By far the most significant reason, however, is the imperative for cost containment, particularly evident in the incentives for limiting inpatient days.

Between 1980 and 1984, the number of Medicare-certified home health agencies doubled, increasing from 2,923 to 5,247. [14] In 1986, expenditures for home health care approximated $14 billion, and are projected to reach $60 billion by the year 2000. [15]

In addition to outpatient surgery and home health care, diversification ventures embrace various "expanded mission" services. With increasing frequency, peripheral programs are being introduced within the framework of the health care system, further broadening its biopsychosocial purview. Curing illness and subduing pain, long the raison d'etre of health care, has been joined by health maintenance and enhancement as the field's proper sphere. Growth has been brisk in the number of hospital-operated sports medicine clinics, health clubs and wellness programs. [16] Among a diverse array of specialty services are programs designed for women's health, adult day care, psychiatric day care, and family planning.

III. A Generalized Approach to ADS

In most cases, ventures in alternative delivery systems involve three parties: (1) sponsors; (2) providers; and (3) purchasers. Generally, in any ADS venture, the sponsors will take the lead in the formulation of proposals and in developing the details of organizational structure, service package, financial plan, and its marketing strategy. The sponsor may be a freestanding entity, such as an insurance carrier or entrepreneur, or it may be a hospital, a group of physicians, or even an employer or labor union.

As the case reports will show, most ADS development proceeds through several phases: (1) the preliminary phase; (2) the feasibility study; (3) the development or planning phase; and (4) the operational phase. Each phase engages the efforts of the three players: sponsor, provider, and purchaser.

1) Preliminary Phase

In the preliminary phase the idea of an ADS venture is broached and a discussion is introduced concerning the justification or need, as perceived by sponsor, provider, or purchaser. Options are considered and tentative goals are established and analyzed. Consideration is given to the resources necessary for achieving those goals, and to the type of sponsorship (e.g., solo or joint venture) that seems best in the situation.

2) Feasibility Study

If the preliminary discussion elicits a broad base of support and sufficient resources appear available to underwrite the venture, a feasibility study generally follows. This phase may be characterized as strategic assessment, inasmuch as it entails analysis of a number of specific elements that have critical bearing on the success of the alternative delivery system.

The feasibility study examines the internal and external environments necessary to support the ADS venture. Internal assessment includes analysis of a number of items, such as the corporate structure of the venture and the cooperation of professional providers (i.e., their willingness to enter into a partnership, their attitude toward this type of ADS, and their position on fees and utilization review). The internal assessment also includes analysis of financial requirements such as start-up costs, sources of capital, and operating costs. Finally, it examines available staff and facilities, the organization of the venture, and the legal aspects of the undertaking.

The external assessment takes a wider view of the venture, analyzing matters such as the market for the plan or service--the demographics of the target population and the pool of potential purchasers. It also considers the competitors for the target group and existing alternative delivery systems and their market penetration.

3) Development (Planning) Phase

If the feasibility study is sufficiently encouraging, the development (or planning) phase is undertaken. This phase, more concrete than the earlier ones, involves design of the product and negotiation of the set of relationships among sponsors, purchasers, and providers--which may involve formulation of a set of incentives for physicians, selection of physicians, and the drafting and signing of contracts. Selective contracting-- that is, negotiations among sponsor, purchaser, and provider--is a central part of this phase.

The reorientation of the purchaser-provider relationship has made provider marketing an issue. What ought to be emphasized in a sponsor's marketing campaign? What are the most important selective contracting considerations for the purchaser? Of course, price, quality, and access are important elements for both sponsor and purchaser. (According to one expert, the major consideration is the financial arrangement for both inpatient and outpatient services.) Other aspects are the scope of services and utilization review standards.

In summary, the development phase involves the creation of an organizational structure, and the resolution of matters of staffing, administration, policy making, financing, budgeting, legality, service package, facilities, marketing, and utilization review.

4) Operational Phase

When the service package and agreements are in place and commitments between sponsors and providers have been established with the signing of contracts, the operational phase begins. The ADS begins implementation of its marketing plan, the provision of medical services, and the monitoring of data. Kress and Singer identify three discrete periods in the operational phase: the gear-up period, in which preparations are made for providing services to enrollees; the early operational period, when enrollment is adequate to support the venture; and full-operation, when the break-even point is passed. [17]

IV. Where Does ADS Go From Here?

1) Further growth and new options

On at least one matter the experts appear to be in complete agreement: alternative delivery systems are rapidly replacing traditional fee-for-service indemnification. (Indeed, some observers see the indemnity business as moribund.) Only the rate of change is open to debate: some experts predict a national enrollment of 50 percent in ADS by 1990, and others expect 65 percent of the U.S. population by 1995. [18, 19] According to Ellwood, virtually everyone who is insured will soon be drawn into some kind of price-competitive alternative delivery system. [20]

Aside from growth, what scenarios does the future hold for ADS? An increasingly strong tendency in health coverage emphasizes options: a flexible benefits package for consumers that includes the indemnity choice, a PPO, and an HMO. Most major insurance carriers now feature this triple-option package, offering consumers the convenience of one-stop shopping; experts predict that in ten years these carriers will control the managed care market. What particular package will emerge as the "winner" in the years ahead? According to one observer, in a price-driven market "the most likely health care financing and delivery system of the future will be an HMO and a regionally based multi-hospital system combined to maximize efficiencies and economies of scale."[21] In addition to the cost savings gained by horizontal integration, vertical diversification of services offers a further competitive advantage.

Already a Darwinian winnowing of the weaker and less adaptable health care organizations is occurring, and unless dramatic regulatory changes emerge from Washington, the ability of providers to compete on the basis of price will be fundamental to survival. We are witnessing price wars among competing providers--recently, in Philadelphia, at least a half dozen managed care plans solicited enrollees--a weeding out process that will leave intact the most efficient and effective operations. In 1986-87, growing competition in the HMO industry generated substantial losses and squeezed profits. In the view of some experts this indicates the onset of a major shakeout in which dozens of HMOs will become takeover targets. "Supermeds" (huge national corporations that combine hospitals, physicians, and insurance) may come to dominate a larger share of the market, while money-losing services such as charity care, teaching, and research could be further hard-pressed. While some experts expect a handful of supermeds to control the majority of the health care system by the turn of the century, others dispute the ongoing competitive struggle implied by this scenario. Ellwood, for example, recently scaled back his forecast of continued competition, and now sees a national health insurance plan as "likely within the next five to ten years. "[22]

According to most experts, in the future we will see a blurring of different kinds of managed care systems--HMOs, PPOs, fee-for-service medicine subject to utilization review. Certainly, we may expect to see a continuing search for more efficient, less expensive modes of care. As cost differences begin to narrow, quality of care will become an increasingly important factor. What should emerge is a competitive environment in which quality joins cost as the basis for consumer choice. It seems safe to predict that the delivery system that best balances quality assurance with cost containment will be the most successful in the years ahead. [23]

2) Social Responsibility in a Competitive Environment

What does this transition to a business-oriented frame of reference implied by ADS suggest about the health manager's social responsibility? Where "market share" is the dominant motivating principle in a provider's decision to diversify with ADS, the development and marketing of superfluous products may be a consequence. Moreover, in addition to created demand, a competitive environment will foster duplication of services, some reduction of funds for education and research, and neglect of the problems of the indigent.

As to the last effect, efforts to palliate the health conditions of the poor by means of managed care have been only partially successful; currently, our nation has 37 million uninsured citizens, and managed care plans serve but a handful of this population. Among the reasons given by HMO administrators for their reluctance to enroll Medicaid recipients are "high rates of turnover in Medicaid eligibility status, high risks of adverse selection, and low Medicaid payment rates."[24]

Even for those individuals enrolled in alternative delivery plans, "undercare" may be one risk of membership; managed care may mean less care if HMOs impose on member physicians powerful disincentives to dispense treatment. One critic voices a frequent complaint in the strongest possible terms, arguing that the HMO manager's strategy is to "attract subscribers who will not use services, to avoid enlisting those who might, and to extrude those who become sick."[25] Quite naturally, many physicians oppose the HMO concept, some for the best of reasons (e.g., constraints imposed on patient advocacy), others from a simple financial calculation. In spite of physicians' attempts to resist the growth of HMOs, surveys find that "their ranks are thin, their funds short, and their spirits wilting. The HMOs are simply rolling over them."[26]

Although competition in health care has been promoted as an idea whose time has come, it may yet give way to greater federal intervention if certain problems such as the growing number of uninsured and AIDS victims cannot be resolved through the private sector. The likelihood of this will increase under a more liberal administration in Washington. Whether power is conservative or liberal, however, ensuring that the lower tier of our health care system offers adequate access and quality to the indigent and elderly ought to be a priority concern for all of us. Toward this end, deliberation on the ethics of ADS entrepreneurialism-- particularly in assessing whether diversification activities fit into the provider's health care mission--may be as much an imperative in the work of the health care manager as the day-to-day decisions made by physicians as they assess the limits of treatment.

V. References

1. Gary J. Rahn. "Becoming Involved." In Hospital-Sponsored Health Maintenance Organizations: Issues for Decision Makers. Gary J. Rahn, ed. American Hospital Association: American Hospital Publishing Inc., 1987, p. 3.

2. Medical Benefits, June 15, 1987.

3. American Medical Care and Review Association survey, December 1986.

4. Medicine and Health Perspectives. May 25, 1987.

5. Paul M. Ellwood. "Alternative Delivery Systems: Health Care on the Move." In Alternative Delivery Systems, Norbert Goldfield and Seth Goldsmith, eds. Rockville, MD: Aspen Systems Corporation, 1987, pp. 1-4.

6. Jeff Goldsmith. Can Hospitals Survive? The New Competitive Health Care Market. Homewood, IL: Dow-Jones Irwin, 1981.

7. Modern Healthcare. June 5, 1987, p. 118.

8. Dale Cowan. Preferred Provider Organizations. Rockville, MD: Aspen Publishers Inc., 1984, p. 5.

9. Modern Healthcare. June 5, 1987, p. 118.

10. Environmental Assessment Overview. The American Hospital Association, 1987.

11. Outreach, The American Hospital Association, March-April, 1986.

12. Medicine and Health Perspectives, May 25, 1987.

13. Modern Healthcare. June 5, 1987, pp. 148-54.

14. Connie Evashwick. "Home Health Care: Current Trends and Future Opportunities." In Alternative Delivery Systems. Goldfield and Goldsmith, eds. Rockville, MD: Aspen Systems Corporation, 1987, pp. 5-18.

15. Medicine and Health, McGraw-Hill, June 8, 1987.

16. Modern Health Care. June 5, 1987, p. 138.

17. John Kress and James Singer. HMO Handbook. Rockville, MD: Aspen Systems Corporation, 1975.

18. Samuel Tibbitts and Dennis Strum. "Looking Forward: The Future of PPOs." In The New Health Care Market. Homewood, IL: Dow Jones-Irwin, 1985, pp.934-46.

19. Michie Hunt. "Managed Care in the 1990s." Health Care Strategic Management, December 1985, pp. 20-24.

20. Paul M Ellwood. "Multisystem Health Care Entities on the Skids, Says Ex-Enthusiast." Medical World News. July 13, 1987.

21. Michie Hunt. "Managed Care in the 1990s." Health Care Strategic Management. December 1985, pp. 20-24.

22. Paul M. Ellwood. "Alternative Delivery Systems: Health Care on the Move." In Alternative Delivery Systems, Goldfield and Goldsmith, eds. Rockville, MD: Aspen Systems Corporation, 1987, pp. 1-4.

23. The Future of Healthcare: Changes and Choices.Arthur Andersen & Co., and The American College of Healthcare Executives: Chicago, 1987

24. Rick Curtis. "The Role of State Government in Assuring Access to Care." Inquiry. 23(3), 1986, pp. 277-85.

25. William Anderson. "HMOs' Incentives: a Prescription for Failure." The Wall Street Journal. Jan. 2, 1987.

26. Rhonda Rundle. "Doctors Who Oppose the Spread of HMOs are Losing Their Fight." The Wall Street Journal. October 6, 1987.

Part Two: Cases

I.   Introduction to HMO Case Studies

The HMO case studies presented here offer different perspectives on hospital/physician contractual negotiations. "Negotiating Contracts with Health Maintenance Organizations and Preferred Provider Organizations" describes a highly competitive environment in which numerous area hospitals attempt to protect shrinking market share by contracting with local HMOs and PPOs. In what one would term the preliminary phase, the author presents an account of various needs: (1) the pressure for Mission Hospital to become involved with alternative delivery systems, (2) the necessary process of sorting through the multitude of alternative delivery systems, and (3) the requirement of some means to evaluate various HMOs and PPOs. In the feasibility study, a checklist of important features is discussed and a profile of each ADS is made. Contracts are drawn up and signed in the operational phase.

The second case, "Factors Involved in Negotiating a Contractual Relationship Between an HMO and a Community Hospital," presents an approach to contracting from a different perspective--that of the HMO which must enlist the services of a community hospital and physicians. Like the first case report, this describes a situation in which a need emerges from shifting market conditions. It also presents decision making based on the evaluation of critical features, such as scope of services, costs, and community attitudes toward the institution. Key to the feasibility study is the analysis of the complex components in the decision to terminate relations with a current provider hospital and frame a contract with a new one. As a part of this analysis, the superiority of the 600 bed facility over the 140 bed hospital in terms of financial and quality considerations is presented in convincing detail.

The third case, "Development of a Rural Health Maintenance Organization," deals not with the complexities of selection and negotiation by independent parties, but with the creation of an alternative delivery system from available resources. In the preliminary phase, the need for an independent HMO emerges from the exclusion of rural health care providers (as voting members) by urban-based HMO plans. From their base in an existing cooperative, the rural providers embark on a feasibility study; a task force is appointed which assumes responsibility for development of the HMO. Expense and enrollment projections are made and service agreements are signed with hospitals and physicians. (The physicians' vehicle for participation is an independent practice association.)

Negotiating Contracts with Health Maintenance
Organizations and Preferred Provider Organizations

Organization Information

Mission Hospital is a 353 bed, non-profit, community general hospital. It was established in the late 1960s by a group of physicians who felt that the long-established hospital where they practiced was not meeting the health needs of the community. The primary service area of Mission Hospital, which includes the suburban areas around the central city, reaches approximately 600,000 people, while the immediate service area reaches 150,000. The city is an expanding "high-tech" center with light industry.

The competitive environment for hospitals in the metropolitan area is intense. There are eight institutions, of which six are 280 beds or larger. All the hospitals are not-for-profit except one, which is a small Humana institution. In addition, the city has become crowded with alternative delivery systems during the past 18 months. Currently, more than 10 PPOs and HMOs are attempting to establish themselves in the community. The impact that these alternative systems have on patient-physician loyalties is great, and is the central reason for the battle for market share.

Gist of the Problem

The newly appointed administrator of Mission Hospital was faced with a rapidly changing marketplace. For numerous reasons, the city where the hospital had prospered over the last decade was in the midst of a war among 10 HMOs and PPOs, which were attempting to carve out their share of the market. Each HMO or PPO had approached the hospital in the hope of establishing a provider relationship with discounted rates. The problem facing Mission hospital management was to develop a strategy for dealing with the HMOs and PPOs and a methodology to select and negotiate with various alternative delivery system organizations.

Description of the Problem

For the past five years, Mission Hospital has prospered in an unregulated Sunbelt state. Two years ago the business climate began to change when a broad range of HMOs and PPOs, from the local medical society to investor-owned national firms, tried to get a foothold in the area.

As the representatives of the HMOs launched their organizing activities, the other hospitals in the community began jockeying for position and showed a willingness to discuss discounts with the organizations. In some cases, the possibility of a joint venture was explored. Before long, difficulties generated by competition among physicians and hospitals began to develop. For Mission Hospital, however, the major problem was the complexity of sorting through alternative delivery system options and selecting those that would be most cost-effective.

The need to establish relationships with alternative delivery systems became more acute in light of the declining patient days experienced under DRGs. While the hospital continued to lead in occupancy, it experienced nearly a 20% drop in census following the introduction of the prospective payment system. Moreover, tension increased among the hospitals when they realized that the once stable physician-patient relationship was being changed dramatically as employers encouraged their employees to consider alternative delivery plans. The need to protect market share by providing deeply discounted services began to weigh heavily on the minds of all the local hospital managers.

The most notable problem facing Mission Hospital in this rapidly changing market was the fact that neither the hospital nor the physicians in the community had experienced the need to negotiate with alternative delivery systems. The traditional practice of medicine was deeply entrenched, and all parties were finding it difficult to make concessions to outside organizations to change payment mechanisms.

Administrative Decision

It was necessary for Mission Hospital to evaluate each alternative delivery system proposal and to make decisions regarding the creation of relationships with the various entities. A checklist of HMO/PPO elements was established so that the principal issues involved in making a decision could be addressed in an orderly fashion. Such an analysis lends itself to a weighted comparison; the administrator found, however, that applying numerical weightings to these items was difficult and could lead one to a false conclusion. A better approach is to establish an HMO or PPO "profile" which would give the hospital a good grasp of the benefits and costs of an ongoing association. A discussion of each item in the checklist follows:

1) Patient Origin Study

Since the primary purpose of involvement with alternative delivery systems is to generate patients and protect market share, it is essential that the current and anticipated projections of patients be carefully studied. Zip-code data should be analyzed to determine where employees and their families are located. Assumptions must be made regarding the ability of the plan to create financial incentives that redirect patient flow to the contracting hospital's physicians and facilities. Physician office locations are crucial in this regard: Unless there are a sufficient number of entry points in the prospective service areas, the hospital will be unable to bring new patients into the system. Obviously, future growth and future directions of the plan are also important. If the plan intends to market vigorously in a growing area, its long term benefits to the hospital could be significant.

2) Physician Support

Physician support of the plan is crucial. While the main concerns initially are fee schedules, most physicians are willing to consider any reasonable alternative system as long as the fees are competitive with their usual and customary rates. Thus, an essential concern for a contracting hospital is the level of physician satisfaction with the approved fee program. In some cases, plans favor certain specialties at the expense of others; therefore, it is necessary to address fees for all major users. Unless a contracting hospital can establish a strong multi-specialty network of physicians with good geographic distribution of offices in the primary service area of the plan, it should not proceed with a contract. In some cases, interested physicians may encourage the hospital to consider an ADS.

The organizational framework of the plan can also have great influence on the level of physician participation. Some physicians find the more rigid closed-panel plans to be too limiting and controversial. Others find that "gatekeeper models" (plans where the primary physicians control all specialist referrals) are also undesirable. The physicians' perception of the overall plan design and their bias regarding the alternative delivery systems may dramatically affect their decision to participate. In the final analysis, the physicians' decisions will depend very much on how concerned they are that their current patient base will be affected adversely by the financial incentives which the ADS introduces into their practice patterns.

3) Board Approval

Obviously, the Board cannot approve a contract until it has been finalized and is ready for presentation. On the other hand, it would be very wasteful to engage in hours of negotiations only to learn that the Board finds the entire concept to be objectionable. Thus, it is suggested that preliminary discussions take place at the Board or executive committee of the Board, so that a general direction can be established for the administration to pursue. Some Boards have gone so far as to establish a maximum allowable discount which they will approve prior to beginning any detailed negotiations. Whether or not the Board actually reviews and approves the final contract is an internal issue.

4) Program Control

Plans differ a great deal in the amount of control which they will allow providers to have. In some cases, an advisory board of physicians is part of the plan, lending assistance in developing fees and carrying out utilization review policies. Other plans, particularly those of larger national companies, are unwilling to yield any control to outsiders and only allow for superficial involvement by providers. The topic of investment possibilities for providers should be addressed with the ADS; in many cases, it is very attractive to have physicians in hospitals participating in a plan as actual investors. In this case, obviously, investors have significant say in the management of the plan.

5) Performance Record

The track record of any plan and its management team is a good indicator of the likelihood of future success; if the management team is new and has never organized or operated a plan, the possibility of success is, of course, less than that which attaches to an experienced management team. The company's ability to succeed in a new market is proportional to the development of its program in other cities.

6) Current Employers Now Affiliated with Related Companies

In cases where an insurance company is involved in an associated HMO or PPO, providers should pay careful attention to the employers now associated with that company because of the likelihood that over time they will be customers of the ADS plan.

7) Plan Image

This primarily affects the medical community involved in providing care. The image of the HMO or PPO can vary greatly depending on the parent organization. For example, a local hospital or medical society not-for-profit program is likely to be regarded as quite different from a national for-profit corporation. The ability to encourage participation from medical staff may very well hinge on their perceived image of the company.

8) Exclusivity

Since it is unrealistic to expect that an HMO or PPO would limit itself to one group of physicians and one hospital, it is essential that participating hospitals understand the size, quality, and specialties of the hospital network and the future plans to include more hospitals in the program. While it is important that an effective accessible network of providers be established, too many hospitals or physicians in the system will frustrate efforts of providers to gain new market share. Providers discount their services in the hope of gaining new business and increased volume; if the participating patients are divided among too many providers, the purpose of the plan is defeated.

9) Provider Involvement with the Operation of the Plan

Some plans are very demanding in terms of the amount of time and work they require of providers. Typical jobs which hospitals and physicians become involved in are utilization review, physician contracting, and even marketing. Hospitals should evaluate the actual cost associated with these responsibilities when considering a relationship. It is suggested they be contractually identified and understood before proceeding with a plan.

10) Financial Resources

Establishing a PPO or HMO can be surprisingly expensive. Total costs may vary from hundreds of thousands of dollars to millions. Providers should review the plan's ability to finance the venture before establishing a relationship.

11) Reimbursement Issues

Simply put, the hospital attempting to evaluate the financial impact of an HMO must be able to compare reimbursement for a given patient population with the cost for delivery of service. Unfortunately, the hospital is frequently unable to make a precise comparison on these issues and may be forced to make a decision based on faulty assumptions. For example, it may be difficult to even determine the type of patients that will be associated with the HMO/PPO, as well as the severity of illness of this population. Obviously, if the cost of delivering care is based on a certain mix of patients within a certain specialty, and if the cost turns out to be something entirely different, the profitability of the service may be changed entirely. If the HMO is large, however, a provider can feel more self-assured that the demand for hospital services may closely approach the norm for similar age-adjusted patient groupings. In some cases, an ADS may have specific patient data regarding its case mix. If the payment mechanism is based on a prospective payment system, miscalculating the severity of patient illness could be financially devastating. If specific patient data is unavailable, it may be helpful to use internal information from another group for evaluation purposes.

12) Hospital-Based Physicians

The issue of compensation for hospital-based physicians can be very difficult, since they often represent essential services that are relatively insignificant to the HMO from a financial point of view. A typical approach to these hospital-based services (e.g., radiology, pathology, anesthesiology) would be to include hospital-based professional components in an overall capitated prospective payment scheme. This would allow the ADS to limit the total dollar commitment to these physicians to a per diem factor and remove the incentive for the physicians to overutilize services. Furthermore, it would eliminate the need for burdensome billing of the physician fees associated with these services.

Unfortunately, since the hospital is forced to secure contracts with these essential services, the negotiations over fees can be extremely challenging--particularly if the physicians perceive the HMO as an objectionable delivery system.

13) Billing Systems

Surprisingly enough, the administration of these uniquely designed reimbursement programs can raise havoc in the hospital's billing office. One problem is that these arrangements become extremely difficult to automate in the business office and often require manual billing. While this issue may seem small, it should not be overlooked in the negotiation process.

14) Contract Terms

If a provider is attractive to the ADS, the hospital will probably be negotiating a contract with a fast termination clause; 30 or 60 day notice requirements are not unusual. On the other hand, hospitals with little leverage against the ADS may be faced with a one year or even five year contract which stipulates rate review at certain intervals. Clearly, from a hospital point of view, it is advisable to negotiate the shortest "out" possible.

In conclusion, the administrator of the hospital who was confronted by an endless variety of HMOs and PPOs organized his alternative plans into a list which highlighted the important elements of each relationship. By making a careful comparison, the administration could draw important conclusions regarding the attractiveness of each plan.

The alternative to this organized analysis would be to do a superficial evaluation, or no evaluation at all, before establishing a provider contract. Typical pitfalls of failing to do a careful evaluation may include the discovery that a hospital has no physician support, no board support, or reimbursement that falls far short of anticipated levels of revenue.

The primary obstacle that the administrator of the hospital faced was constant pressure from his medical staff and board to conclude negotiations and establish a contract as quickly as possible. It should be noted that negotiations of this type are complex and lengthy, but it should also be noted that a hasty conclusion leading to a poor contract will be a source of regret.

Results

The administrator of Mission Hospital applied the methods described above, completed his assessment, and ultimately contracted with three HMOs and four PPOs in his community over a four month period. Since the establishment of the contracts, 18 months have passed, and most of the contracts have resulted in successful sponsor-provider relationships; in some cases, the contracts have actually been renewed and have begun their second year. In one particular case, however, the contract proved to be poorly structured and resulted in a hastily developed interim contract and, ultimately, termination. Much can be learned from this failure. A major difficulty was generated by a lack of physician support, particularly in the case of hospital-based physicians. Further, assumptions regarding patient mix and severity were wrong, and prospective payment arrangements resulted in inadequate reimbursement. A termination of contract was the only reasonable course for the hospital.

Factors Involved in Negotiating a Contractual Relationship
Between an HMO and a Community Hospital

Organization Information

     Secure Care -- a small, not-for-profit health maintenance organization--has 24,000 enrollees and provides primary care services to them at three different health centers in a metropolitan area. The specialty and hospital services offered by the HMO are arranged through contracts with community providers. In its seven-year history, the HMO has undergone three changes of ownership and recently was acquired by a large, well-established not-for-profit HMO. Secure Care retained its identity and made the transition through the acquisition with a minimum of turmoil for enrollees, management, and medical staff.

     The metropolitan area served by Secure Care is a community of approximately 170,000 people, with a county-wide population of 350,000. The health care facilities in the community include two large tertiary referral hospitals, one of 300 beds and the other 600. Both are teaching hospitals and have established good reputations as institutions providing high quality, tertiary services. Three community hospitals operate within the metropolitan area: a 140 bed facility in the downtown area, a 250 bed operation to the north of town, and a 120 bed organization to the east of the downtown area. Other facilities include a Veterans Administration hospital and several freestanding community health clinics, two home health agencies, and several nursing homes.

Gist of the Problem

     In its seven-year history, the HMO subject of this report had not developed a preferential relationship with a particular hospital. Upon expiration of a contract with the 140 bed hospital, Secure Care was faced with the task of negotiating a new agreement for hospital services.

     Although most HMOs must work out contractual arrangements with specialists and hospitals, no standard guidelines exist for handling such negotiations. These arrangements are heavily influenced by the individual nature of the HMO itself, as well as by competitors, physicians' attitudes, the financial stability and attitudes of community hospitals, and a variety of other issues that make each of these negotiations a unique exercise.

Description of the Problem

Hospitalization is always the largest category of expense for an HMO, whether it provides hospital care itself or purchases care in the community. Negotiation for services is one of the most important and complex matters facing an HMO, as it involves a number of subjective variables in addition to cost considerations. Moreover, the decision by an HMO to change hospitals introduces the further complexity of new professional relationships, and quite often involves political consequences. Thus, negotiation is perhaps the most significant activity facing an HMO, and has more to do with its continued financial stability and reception in the community than anything else it can do through marketing programs, public relations efforts, or advertising campaigns.

As mentioned, Secure Care had not developed a preferential relationship with any hospital. Because of custom and usual physician preference, the plan's physicians had always worked as a group in one of the hospitals--although they had changed preferences several times over the seven-year history. The volume they generated accounted for less than 50 percent of the total patient days for the plan's enrollment. The balance was referred by specialists in the community or was generated through emergency room admissions.

Prior to the acquisition of the plan by the parent organization, Secure Care had entered into a per diem arrangement with the 140 bed hospital. This agreement accounted for 40 percent of the plan's patient days, and involved those patients admitted by the plan's own medical staff. Most of the remaining admissions, principally specialty referrals, were directed to the 600 bed teaching facility, with a small percentage going to the 300 bed hospital. As the expiration of the agreement with the 140 bed hospital approached, negotiations were started for the following year. Several factors led the organization to reconsider the benefits of retaining this contractual relationship:

1)   The actual charges of the hospital were approximately $100 per day higher than the charges of the 600 bed tertiary facility. Thus, the organization had to provide a large (22%) discount to reach a level similar to the non-discounted charges of the 600 bed facility.

2)   The hospital commission in this state, which has power to review budgets and determine rates, was taking an active role in critically reviewing such discount arrangements.

3)   Specialty physicians in the community had strong feelings regarding the smaller facility and often actively resisted being asked to perform surgery there. All three hospitals are within a ten-block radius and the physicians usually preferred admitting their patients either to the 300 bed or 600 bed hospital.

4)   Since approximately half of the plan's patients were admitted to the 600 bed facility, it seemed an appropriate time to consider the convenience and efficiencies to be gained by consolidating all admissions in one hospital.

5)   Finally, although the 600 bed facility had never entered into any preferential contract with the HMO, the medical staff and administration indicated that they were favorably disposed to negotiate with the new entity.

All of the hospitals in the area had approached Secure Care to discuss possible contractual relationships. The HMO management decided to concentrate its negotiation efforts on the 140 bed hospital and the 600 bed facility. The 300 bed tertiary facility had not responded to requests for discussion; the hospital to the north of the city was inconvenient for large portions of the metropolitan area; the community hospital to the east, in addition to its geographical inconvenience, lacked a full range of services.

The focus of discussion in these negotiations was the financial implications of continuing with the two hospitals, as opposed to consolidating all hospitalization in the 600 bed tertiary facility. Significant factors that entered the decision-making process were:

1)   scope of services provided by each institution;

2)   amount of change/disruption that would involve enrollees and medical staff if a major change in hospitals was undertaken;

3)   the benefits to the HMO in reduced charges under either hospital arrangement;

4)   perception of quality, scope of services, and working relationships as expressed by specialists with whom the plan has referral arrangements;

5)   future financial stability and impact of major expansion projects on rates in both hospitals;

6)   availability of capacity for the plan's hospital needs;

7)   attitudes toward both institutions as expressed by business leaders, benefits managers, and enrollee population.

In-depth discussions were held with hospital administrators and medical staff leaders at both institutions over a three-month period. Both hospitals had received approval from their respective Boards to enter into negotiations with the HMO. Secure Care's Board of Directors had approved the plan to negotiate new arrangements with either one or both of the community hospitals.

Administrative Decision

After several discussions with representatives from both hospitals, the decision was made to consolidate all admissions in the 600 bed tertiary facility--a complex determination involving several factors. First, although the plan's physicians and members did not indicate dissatisfaction with quality of care at the 140 bed facility, they did reveal a high opinion of the care at the 600 bed hospital. Clearly, this respect within the community offered a public relations advantage.

A second major issue concerned the financial arrangements with each hospital. The 600 bed facility had Hospital Commission approved charges that were very similar to the published charges for the 140 bed hospital, despite the fact that the 600 bed facility had all the high cost tertiary services associated with a major referral center. The services included cardiac surgery, neurosurgery, obstetrical services, neonatal intensive care, psychiatric services, and sophisticated intensive care and cardiac care units. None of these services were provided at the 140 bed facility. During discussions, it became clear that the 140 bed hospital would be required to increase rates by a significant amount during the coming year because of declining occupancy and the need to depreciate a recent expansion project. Again, they were forced to offer a discount in the range of 15 to 20 percent in order to be competitive with non-discounted charges at the 600 bed facility.

A third major factor affecting the decision was the handling of Medicare patient days. Secure Care offered a supplemental Medicare plan, covering all outpatient services, paid for directly by Medicare to community hospitals. It is able to direct the Medicare enrollees to a designated facility, thereby increasing volume and helping to spread fixed costs; moreover, the HMO is able to assume the hospital's DRG risk by becoming the payor for its Medicare population.

Secure Care asked each hospital to provide it with costs and charges on the Medicare patients that the plan had directed to it but for whom the hospital had received reimbursement from Medicare. The results were surprising. The Medicare patients admitted to the 140 bed hospital generated charges of approximately $775 per patient day, while those admitted to the 600 bed tertiary facility generated charges of $522 per day. Thus, even though these were considered general, adult medicine patients, they were high-cost patients in the 140 bed facility, but patients of average cost in the 600 bed hospital.

The HMO projected 4500 Medicare patient days out of 11,000 days for the plan as a whole in 1984. When the 600 bed facility became aware of the magnitude of the patient days and also more familiar with the upcoming DRG reimbursement rates, they proposed to the HMO a package that included the impact of the Medicare patients on its overall volume and subsequent rate structure. The arrangement to provide cost reductions to the HMO's non-Medicare patient days consisted of two elements: First, the additional volume of all patient days was sufficient to allow the hospital to recalculate charges and reduce rates to all payors; thus, Secure Care received a reduction in charges that was available to all other hospital patients as well. Second, the other portion of the charge determination was based on the difference between the hospital's DRG reimbursement and the costs of the HMO's Medicare patient days. Thus, the incentive to Secure Care was to control the costs of its Medicare patient days and apply this cost differential in reducing charges to its non-Medicare patient days.

The effect of making these calculations was large enough to reduce the charges from the 600 bed hospital below the per diem that could be offered by the 140 bed hospital. For the latter, the per diem offered for 1984 was $475; the comparable figure for the 600 bed hospital, after calculations for Medicare days and total volume projections, was $460 per patient day. The Medicare patient days became the critical factor in the decision analysis: They actually helped to reduce overall charges in the 600 bed hospital, as DRG reimbursement rates were higher than actual charges; the opposite was true in the 140 bed hospital. For the 140 bed hospital, the Medicare patients' DRG reimbursement rates were much lower than the hospital's charges for those services.

A fourth area which had significant implications for the HMO, particularly its medical staff, was the relationship of Secure Care with the teaching programs of the tertiary hospital. One of the concerns of any HMO is the potential danger of having patient services directed by residents in teaching programs, where a commitment to cost containment may not exist. Fortunately, discussions with hospital and medical staff representatives, leaders of the residency programs, and residents themselves, revealed that a partnership with an HMO could benefit all parties. The partnership would clearly emphasize the need for cost containment in the physician's determination of clinical appropriateness of services. Cost containment considerations, particularly the financial burden to individual patients, would be emphasized in residency programs.

Another concern was the HMO physicians' enthusiastic support of a family practice residency program at the 140 bed hospital. They were very much interested in creating a similar program at the 600 bed tertiary facility. Finally, these physicians looked forward to the challenge of influencing other physicians' behavior by modeling appropriate relationships between the HMO and residents who were soon to become community practitioners. Thus, a potentially thorny issue became an attractive benefit for all three major parties: the HMO physicians, the hospital, and the residency program.

Results

The financial results for the HMO were approximately $200,000 in reduced hospital costs for the first year of the contract. During the second year, cost savings could exceed $300,000 and approach as much as $400,000. The principal determinants in the second year are growth, subsequent hospital utilization because of such growth, and the difference in costs incurred for Medicare patient days and DRG-based reimbursement to the hospital. The unique factors that contributed to these results bear repeating.

First, normally when DRG-based reimbursement is set at levels lower than a hospital's charges, costs are shifted to other payors. In certain areas of the country, however, where the DRG formulae are based on high-cost states, certain efficient hospitals are able to benefit from the DRG rates. What is most unusual in the case under discussion is that the 600 bed tertiary facility has the lowest charges of the five community hospitals-- the result of a long-standing tradition of providing low cost, comprehensive services to the community. (The 300 bed hospital has charges exceeding $100 per day more than comparable services in the 600 bed facility.) Also, the 600 bed facility has the lowest charges of comparable hospitals across the entire state, as determined by the State Hospital Commission. It would be hard to imagine a similar circumstance in other communities where a full service, tertiary hospital would also be the hospital of lowest cost.

Second, the ability of an HMO to direct its patient population allows it significant leverage when approaching community hospitals. Even though the HMO receives no direct financial benefit from the Medicare population, it is able to manipulate this group to achieve benefits for its non-Medicare population. Many HMOs have not entered into Medicare contractual arrangements because of the high risk involved with this population group. A decision by Secure Care to obtain Medicare enrollees turned out to be a key factor in allowing the plan to achieve substantial cost saving for its non-Medicare population. The magnitude of the utilization characteristics of this group is as follows: the Medicare enrollment is approximately eight percent of the plan's total enrollment, but it accounts for over 40 percent of the plan's hospital days.

Finally, the willingness of Secure Care physicians to participate in teaching programs and the hospital's interest in having HMO physicians "model" for other staff physicians, enhanced the arrangement. Having respected, cost-effective physicians working in the hospital will also help the hospital in its educational programs for physicians new to the DRG-based reimbursement formulae.

The advantages to Secure Care of having an affiliation with a premier hospital facility are substantial. The HMO directs enrollees to use HMO facilities, approved specialists, and designated hospitals; it is incumbent on the HMO, in all aspects of its operation, to continually assure its enrollees that its decisions are appropriate ones. To be sure, HMOs often make arrangements with less than the best physicians available, and often with less than the best hospitals available--a practice that is rationalized in the name of cost containment, but one that is deleterious to the HMO's attractiveness and market penetration in the long run. Secure Care has achieved the best of all possible worlds: it is clearly affiliated with the premier hospital in town and is providing high quality care at the lowest available price. In terms of financial significance, the magnitude of the savings per year ($200,000 to $400,000) is the difference between merely breaking even and producing a margin of 2-3 percent in total revenues. Thus, this decision not only affects the single most expensive category of services for the HMO, but also has the potential of doubling a budget margin of $100,000-$200,000.

The above analysis indicates the complex nature of any arrangement between a community hospital and an HMO. As noted above, it has implications for the entire range of hospital operations. It also has consequences for the relationships between hospital administration and its medical staff--HMOs are not always met with enthusiasm and a community hospital must be prepared to back its decision actively when opposed by influential members of its medical staff. Finally, this HMO-hospital arrangement recognizes both the HMO's concern with the utilization practices of the teaching program, and the influence of responsible, respected physicians on traditional overutilization practices; moreover, the administration may encourage HMO physician involvement in teaching programs and physician education workshops.

The new pressure on community hospitals brought about by DRG-based reimbursement will emphasize the hospital-physician partnership that is at the core of a successful HMO's operation. Many of the techniques employed by an HMO, such as physician selection, peer review, utilization review, and education can be applied to the hospital's need to develop similar programs with its own medical staff.

The benefits to both the 600 bed hospital and Secure Care include reinforcement of the strengths that have made them successful, namely, the hospital's commitment to low cost, high quality services that allow it to remain an outstanding tertiary center, and the HMO's ability to continue to sell a comprehensive benefit at a competitive premium. This arrangement will also allow Secure Care to increase its Medicare marketing activities, further benefiting both the HMO and the community hospital. Significantly, it also allows both organizations to continue to provide socially needed services to the Medicare population.

Development of a Rural Health Maintenance Organization

Organization Information

Walden Hospital is a non-profit facility with 74 acute care beds, owned and operated by a 14 member multi-hospital system located primarily in the Midwest. The population of the city is 10,000 and the primary service area includes 25,000 residents. The majority of the patients come from the city in which Walden Hospital is located and from another city of 5,000 located 18 miles away. Three other non-profit community hospitals lie within a 20-mile radius. Five tertiary hospitals are located 40 miles away in a metropolitan area.

Gist of the Problem

Recently, the urban hospitals and physician clinics began to develop four urban-based health maintenance organizations in response to a major policy change in the state legislature relating to health care coverage. Many observers thought that private industry would also seek out HMO coverage for employees. The rural hospitals and physicians did not want to become subservient to an urban-based plan, and so decided to develop their own HMO.

Description of the Problem

In recent years, state legislators have generated a number of provisions concerning the healthcare insurance system, including legislation making it easier to establish HMOs and PPOs. At the same time, the state decided to bid out the health care coverage of its employees, 35,000 of whom are in the service area of Walden Hospital and the surrounding hospitals. The state program was developed using co-payments and deductibles to make it advantageous for the employees to choose an HMO alternative.

In response to these changes, the urban-based hospitals and clinics, either jointly or independently, began to establish HMO plans in order to protect and increase their share of the market. A statewide HMO plan was developed by Blue Cross. None of the HMOs were willing to allow rural hospitals or rural physicians to become substantially involved in the development or operation of their plan; they were to be treated as providers, not as voting participants.

Years earlier, the rural hospitals had formed a rural hospital cooperative to address a number of economic and political issues (e.g., sharing of services, group purchasing). Recently, in response to the pricing practices and projected premium increases of the health insurance companies,

33

the cooperative established a self-insurance program for its employees; the hospitals and their boards jointly established and funded a corporation to create the self-insurance program, a project that involved the sharing of a great deal of information.

In response to the HMO development in the urban area, the rural hospital cooperative called for a meeting of the medical staffs, board members, and representatives from the hospitals who were interested in exploring the feasibility of establishing a rural-based HMO. Discussion centered on recent revisions in the laws, the activities being undertaken by the urban hospitals and clinics, and the potential impact of these changes on the rural hospitals and physicians.

Administrative Decision

Since the option of equitable participation in an urban-based HMO plan was not available, the rural hospitals and physicians decided that if they were to survive and maintain any meaningful control over their operation and practices, they would have to develop a viable alternative to the urban-based HMO plans. This option posed a number of major problems:

1) The rural hospitals were geographically distributed over the entire southwest portion of the state.

2) Although the hospital administrators had worked together before, their medical staffs had not.

3) Because the project was late in getting started, it faced an extremely short timetable of two and a half months to develop the HMO and submit the application, and four additional months to begin operation.

4) The project needed to raise the start-up costs, including consulting fees.

5) The project needed credibility if it was to be successful.

After reviewing and rejecting a number of proposals drawn up by consultants, one of the urban hospitals whose medical staff was establishing an HMO independent of the hospital proposed an arrangement with the cooperative members. The urban hospital had been studying the feasibility of establishing an HMO for five years, and had worked with a nationally known consultant in this effort. The urban hospital offered to make this consultant available to the rural cooperative, and to pay the first $150,000 of development costs. In return, the cooperative would agree to direct all appropriate patient referrals to the hospital for a period of three years. The other urban hospitals made counter proposals, but the original proposal was accepted because it allowed for control of the HMO by rural hospitals and physicians. In addition, the inclusion of the urban hospital also gave credibility to the rural-based HMO.

A task force with representatives from the hospitals and medical staffs assumed responsibility for development of the HMO structure. The physicians were responsible for developing the Independent Practice Associates (IPA) which would serve as the vehicle for physician participation. The executive director of the cooperative served as the coordinator for all of the participants (consultants, hospitals, physicians, lawyers, and accountants).

The hospitals agreed to fund the remaining cost of development (in excess of $150,000) and the other start-up costs associated with the HMO, while the physicians assumed financial responsibility for the IPA. The development of the HMO proceeded with only one major problem: It involved a multi-specialty urban-based clinic which staffed many specialty outpatient clinics operating in the rural area and was a major referral group. The HMO task force learned that this clinic was developing its own HMO, and had assumed that it would fulfill the HMO needs of the rural area. Therefore, it considered the rural-based HMO a competitor.

Because of this clinic's involvement with hospitals and clinics in the rural area, the HMO task force was anxious to have it as a participant in the rural HMO. Intense discussions between the clinic and the HMO went on for a period of months, and the clinic finally decided that the positive impact of its involvement with the rural HMO outweighed the advantages of its direct HMO involvement in the rural area.

The state established the minimum scope of services for HMOs serving its employees. It had agreed to pay 90% of the standard health plan, or the lowest HMO premium, whichever was less. The HMO agreed to pay the hospitals at the last per diem approved by the State Rate Review Committee. The physicians were paid at 95% of the average charge, based on a survey by the IPA of physician charges in the area. Since a majority of the physicians lived in the rural area, the physician reimbursement reflected the lower rural physician incomes rather than the higher urban incomes. While some urban physicians were initially reluctant to accept these lower fees, they agreed to participate upon review of the volume of referrals.

Initially, eleven hospitals and approximately 300 rural and urban-based physicians agreed to be a part of the HMO. Marketing of the rural HMO involved the mailing of HMO literature to all eligible employees, and a number of informational meetings between HMO representatives and state employees. Each hospital and medical staff utilized its community connections to market the HMO to both public and private employers.

In setting the premiums, the HMO task force chose to be realistic in its expense projections and very conservative in its enrollment projections.

Expense projections were based on past experiences of HMOs with which the consultant had been associated; the enrollment figure was estimated at 700. The task force felt that by basing the budget on this conservative enrollment figure, the financial viability of the HMO would be increased.

Results

During the enrollment period, the rural HMO signed approximately 2,700 state employees, almost four times the number that had been projected; at the time of this writing, the HMO has enrolled a total of 6,200 members. The additional enrollees are employees of rural businesses who are realizing the savings of an HMO, while at the same time supporting their local rural medical community. The HMO has signed a total of 21 hospitals and approximately 1,300 physicians. The number of patient days per 1000 is 383 as compared to the budgeted number of 476.

The rural HMO has proven to be a viable alternative to the urban-based HMOs, based on its successful operation thus far. It allows rural patients to remain in rural hospitals when appropriate and to receive quality care at tertiary hospitals at a lower cost when such treatment is necessary. In addition, the HMO structure offers a forum for open discussion between rural hospitals and rural physicians. This improved communication within the rural health community will allow it to keep pace with the changing health care delivery system.

II. Introduction to PPO Case Studies

In each of the following cases, the author describes a competitive health care environment and the need on the part of a provider to protect and enhance market share. Each case presents the evolution of a preferred provider arrangement, from origin of the idea, to planning and implementation.

The first case, "Responding to Market Changes: Evolution of a Preferred Provider Organization," shows the development of a PPO by a hospital. The preliminary phase is considered in some detail here, from the manifest need to control health care costs, to the creation of a coalition of community leaders and representatives from local hospitals, to the definition of a model health care plan. The planning phase entered upon by Lydgate hospital involves design of a competitive plan that meets the specifications of the coalition. Of particular interest in this regard are (1) the efforts of the hospital to be responsive to the specific needs of the area businesses; and (2) the added features (e.g., health education, wellness programs) that give it an advantage over its competitors. According to the author, keys to success for the hospital-sponsored preferred provider organization are "planning, strong board support, and a willingness to take calculated risks."

Cases two and three also describe the development of a hospital-sponsored PPO. "Establishing a Hospital-Based Preferred Provider Organization" is notable for its description of a carefully researched and organized approach to the development of a PPO. The author begins with a description of the competitive environment and the need to retain and improve census levels, then undertakes a feasibility study that addresses three primary questions: (1) Can the service area support a PPO? (2) Can three small for-profit hospitals capture patients from larger not-for-profit competitors? (3) Can a concept as new as a preferred provider organization succeed in a conservative community? Following an extensive period of information gathering, the author embarks on the developmental phase with the preparation of plans for matters such as organizational arrangement, physician enlistment, and marketing strategy. Key to the success of the PPO is an aggressive promotional program involving presentations to businesses, physicians, and the public.

"Preferred Provider Organization Options in a Metropolitan Health Care Market" discusses the development of a hospital-sponsored PPO as a plan distinct in its market segment--one designed for those purchasers not interested in indemnity plans and HMOs. Of particular note here is the extensive feasibility phase: the task force's study includes an assessment of both internal and external elements that bear on the case--from market analysis to utilization review--and also an overview of ownership options. Finally, the criteria vital to organizational success (e.g., physician compatibility, flexibility) are identified and applied to the ADS alternatives, and the decision to purchase a controlling portion of a locally owned PPO follows.

Responding to Market Changes: Evolution of a Preferred Provider Organization

Organization Information

Lydgate Hospital is a 471 bed facility located in a city of approximately 170,000. The city borders another state, and just across the state line is a city of 30,000; a nearby major military installation brings the total area population to 250,000. Lydgate Hospital is the major provider of primary care services for the immediate area and of tertiary services for the entire service area.

The immediate area is currently served by four general hospitals and a specialty surgical hospital. One is a 290 bed hospital affiliated with a religious order, and another is an investor-owned hospital with 252 beds adjacent to the subject hospital. Recently, the investor-owned company opened a 100 bed surgical hospital in the city. Just a few miles away in an adjoining state is a 290 bed county-controlled hospital.

Total inpatient capacity within the immediate community is approximately 1,300. The inpatient occupancy at the five hospitals has fallen during the past 18 months to the point where 500-550 beds lie vacant on any given day. Lydgate Hospital maintains an occupancy rate of approximately 60 percent, which appears to be the highest level in the community. Given these utilization levels, it is little wonder that a high degree of competition among hospitals and physicians has developed.

Gist of the Problem

The problem facing Lydgate Hospital was maintenance and expansion of market share in a marketplace of declining and shifting demand. The business community was earnestly seeking methods of health care cost containment which focused attention on health care providers, but at the same time afforded new opportunities for progressive management. This report examines the development and evolution of a preferred provider organization which was designed to match hospital resources with community demand.

Description of the Problem

In the spring of 1982, amid considerable national debate over the rising cost of health care and local activity with health care alliances, community leaders developed the state's first health care coalition. The chief executive officers of five of the city's most influential businesses formed the steering committee. From the outset, it was determined that the coalition would involve health care providers in an effort to work cooperatively to

38

remedy the many problems contributing to the rising cost of health care. All of the local hospitals became participating members. For several months, the energies of the coalition were concentrated primarily on general education of its membership, particularly on problems associated with the rising cost of health care and the approaches taken by other communities to deal with these problems. Discussions during these months touched on the viability of alternative delivery systems, such as health maintenance organizations and preferred provider organizations.

The management staff of Lydgate Hospital had considered a program which would bind the community to its facilities. A literature review had produced an interesting discovery: in several instances, hospitals had successfully implemented "credit card" programs in which preferred customers were issued cards following a screening of their credit worthiness. Lydgate was in the process of planning a very sophisticated computer system which would enable storage and retrieval of massive numbers of pre-registered patients, and the idea of a pre-registration arrangement tied to some sort of card system presented an interesting possibility. Although this idea appeared workable to the management staff, it did not offer the scope of innovation necessary to obtain competitive advantage.

Through participation in coalition activities, Lydgate Hospital quickly discovered that the businesses were interested in a long-term solution to the health care cost problem for themselves and their employees. They were receptive to the possibility of attaching health education and wellness programming to their solution. Lydgate was seen as the community leader in this area because it had for years operated a medical education program which provided the basis for continuing health education for the community.

One of the first things done by the member firms of the health care coalition was to define a model health care benefit plan. The primary mechanism by which they proposed to reduce their health care cost was to shift the burden of higher deductibles and co-payments to their employees. If the program developed by Lydgate was to be attractive, it would need to consider the burdens being placed on employees.

Administrative Decision

In an effort to respond to changing market conditions, Lydgate Hospital developed a preferred provider organization. Management designed the PPO with great care, so as to address many of the concerns expressed by the local business community. The program was intended to provide a cash discount of up to ten percent to employers, contingent upon increased utilization of the hospital's inpatient facilities. Each participating organization was required to increase its previous year's utilization by ten percent in order to qualify for any level of discount. In practice, the actual discount was staggered depending on annual admissions, and a company achieved the maximum ten percent discount on only a relatively small number of patients at a high utilization level. Most companies would realize only a four to five percent discount on all admissions over a period of one year. To enhance interest in the program, Lydgate offered health education and wellness programs at a nominal fee.

The employee became the special focus of the PPO. Each employee admitted under the program received some added recognition from his/her company, as well as cash discounts upon use of the hospital. For the company and employee, special requirements were established for rapid claim settlement. The card system (mentioned earlier) was incorporated into the program to act as the identifier for the entire system. All participating employers were required to have their employees fill out data sheets which provided the necessary information for pre-registration at our facility and its outlying centers. Each company also agreed to provide the hospital with an opportunity to meet with groups of employees for the purpose of selling the program. In effect, we had created for Lydgate an opportunity for direct marketing to all employees within the participating business.

Specific attention was given to the largest employers within the community, those with more than 500 employees, and for the first six months almost all marketing efforts were directed at those companies. After six months of operation, the PPO had enrolled a half dozen companies. Most companies in the target group were national organizations with local offices, and after many months of effort, we concluded that it would be difficult to get such companies committed to a small local program. We also realized that there was significant opportunity within the small to medium size employer group which made up the bulk of our community. Therefore, plans were initiated to develop a strategy which would allow us to market the same program to smaller employers without compromising our goals.

The new program was introduced by means of heavy media attention, civic club interaction, and hospital-sponsored business men's luncheons. After a year, the PPO included about 30 companies, a number that soon tripled. Currently, the program encompasses some 240 companies with approximately 16,000 employees, bringing the total coverage to 48,000 employees and dependents--approximately one-third of the insured employees in our marketplace.

From the outset, Lydgate Hospital attempted to involve physicians in the PPO. We saw the PPO as a unique opportunity to introduce a leading national trend into our marketplace, and also to develop a physician bond with our facility which had not previously existed. Since we are a medium size community, however, the multiple hospital allegiance among physicians was quite strong. There was reluctance on the part of a relatively conservative medical staff to seek any specific institutional affiliation.

As the PPO grew, it became quite obvious that there was strong community interest in alternative delivery systems, which spurred action on the part of physicians, other hospitals, and insurance companies toward competitive program development. The physicians within the community felt it necessary to develop an organization to preserve their individual practice opportunities. Shortly after the introduction of the PPO, attempts were made by local physicians to consolidate their resources toward some self-serving end. After a year, the first organizational initiative of some 100 physicians was deemed a failure.

A spin-off group of physicians, however, decided the idea was worth pursuing and continued efforts toward development of a physician PPO. The major stumbling block in the development of this organization was the physicians' unwillingness to affiliate with a given institution. Some members of the physician group were the original founders of the hospital run by the religious order; many others had an ownership interest in the investor-owned facility, and several were generally supportive of Lydgate Hospital. Since there was not unity of purpose, even the newly founded physician group had difficulty in formulating any strong plan.

The competing hospitals soon began to realize that the PPO was a competitive force. The hospital run by the religious order responded by offering a discount to Blue Cross for all its subscribers. Hampered by declining market share in our region, Blue Cross jumped at the opportunity and openly promoted this hospital and its discount program. A subsequent analysis of activity at the subject hospital one year later indicated no significant shift in Blue Cross patients. Therefore, one may conclude that this quick-fix attempt by the competing hospital was totally unsuccessful.

The investor-owned hospital had no local program to introduce. However, there had been test marketing of a corporate-level program in three major cities in the southeastern United States. The corporate directors of this program came to our city in the spring of 1984 to talk about the corporation's development of a preferred provider organization and its eventual applicability to our community. This too, we believe, is a direct result of the competitive effect of our PPO. The fact that the corporation did not have the program ready for immediate implementation in our city proved to be counterproductive for them and much to our advantage.

Results

The PPO has provided the foundation for Lydgate Hospital to move into new areas of marketing and program development. Contact with business leaders gave the hospital valuable insight regarding the community's interest in less costly health care. Our discovery of a wide interest in primary care centers provided the impetus to move ahead with the development of a series of such facilities, which eventually will be integrated into the PPO program, with major emphasis given to the needs of the industrial and business community.

The program has evolved to the point where it has broad community recognition and support. During the holiday season, a safe-driving campaign co-sponsored by the local newspaper, a local private psychiatric hospital, and our hospital was conducted. Our focus for the program has been the family, and we have conducted multiple educational programming sessions for the public with either free or nominal admission for PPO members.

Attempts have been made to capitalize on every available opportunity to bring potentially beneficial organizations into the PPO. For example, Lydgate Hospital recently decided to consider contracting with one of the major national firms for the management of its food service operations. As a part of the negotiating process with the competing vendors, each was asked about the willingness of their company to participate as PPO members. In addition, each competing vendor was asked to submit suggestions to the hospital regarding how special benefits from their firms could be made available to PPO members. Though a final selection of the food service management company has not yet been made, two of the companies have made significant proposals that extend benefits to PPO cardholders. One firm which operates restaurants nationwide has proposed to extend a ten percent discount to all PPO card holders who dine at their restaurants. Additionally, marketing to one of the major national pharmaceutical houses with retail outlets resulted in a general agreement that will permit PPO cardholders to purchase pharmaceuticals at cost plus a nominal dispensing fee.

It is obvious that major hospital corporations have significant resources which can be summoned to develop competitive programs similar to ours. However, it is our belief that the major competitive advantage of our program is the ability we have to tailor a program to the specific needs of our community and to alter and enhance the program as market conditions change. Through arrangements such as that with the food service management company, we maintain a significant competitive advantage at the local level. The attractiveness of our program is further enhanced by the fact that we are the only full-service health care provider within the community. Competing facilities, particularly those of major national hospital corporations which provide limited services, have found it very difficult to enter into contractual relationships with businesses when they are unable to provide a full range of services to their employees.

The continuing success of the program has now reached a point where a large number of medical staff members have expressed interest in direct affiliation with Lydgate's PPO. The program has been structured to allow physician participation under the stipulation that they commit to a utilization management plan and peer review in exchange for inclusion in the hospital's marketing program. There is obviously an expectation of increased patient base through this affiliation. The hospital has also structured some tangible benefits such as marketing, purchasing, and personnel services as part of the advantage of being a participating physician.

We believe this alliance will provide the necessary resources to deal with the increasing demands of local business and industry. Although many of the local health care coalition businesses are participating members of the PPO, there has continued to be a desire on the part of the health care coalition leadership to maintain total independence from any single institution. Although it is unlikely that any hospital will become the exclusive provider of services to the business community, it is our belief that through physician affiliation with our program, we can become the chief provider of services.

The success of this program is best documented by the increased level of utilization obtained by the first of the companies to participate in the program for a full year. To date, only two major companies have completed one full year under the program, and their levels of inpatient utilization of our facility increased 305 percent and 150 percent. The total discounts provided to the companies averaged five percent. The increase in hospital revenue from these two companies alone amounted to $276,000. After one year of operation, overall hospital revenues were increased by $460,000 because of the PPO. Conservative estimates at this point would place additional hospital revenue for the second year at $3 million, which can be directly attributed to the PPO program.

The success of the PPO program clearly demonstrates that proactive and progressive management teams in public hospitals can compete successfully with investor-owned hospitals and private, non-profit facilities. The obvious keys to success are planning, strong board support, and a willingness to take calculated risks.

Organization Information

Unity Care, a group of three for-profit hospitals with a total of 253 beds, is operated by a chain in a community with a stable population of 200,000; a state university adds 20,000 to this number, and a military base another 10,000. The basis for a relatively strong economy is diversification: in addition to the state university and military base, there is oil exploration and production, manufacturing, and agriculture. Unemployment has consistently been below the national average.

The medical community is highly competitive. Seven acute care hospital facilities with a combined total of 1500 beds are located in the city. In addition, there is a psychiatric hospital, six urgent care centers, a free-standing surgical center, and an outpatient rehabilitation center. Four hundred thirty-six medical doctors and 28 osteopathic physicians make a physician to population ratio of one to 459. The bed ratio per thousand population is 7.5.

In view of the heavy concentration of available physicians and beds, health care organizations must constantly search for ways to retain and improve census levels. In the last twelve months, patient days at Unity Care have declined 15 percent. All area acute facilities have experienced the effects of DRGs and the pressure to remain under the reimbursement limits established under the Medicare program.

Gist of the Problem

Because of the competitive environment, the declining patient day census, and the lack of any managed care systems such as health maintenance organizations and preferred provider organizations in the area, the case writer and his colleagues made a decision to establish a preferred provider organization based in Unity Care.

Description of the Problem

The first part of our work was to determine if the market could support a PPO. We also had to know if three relatively small for-profit institutions and related companies could pull patients away from the larger, more established not-for-profit neighboring institutions. Further, we wished to know if a concept as new as a PPO could be marketed effectively in a very conservative community. Resistance was expected from our competitors, since establishment of a PPO would be viewed as a direct threat to them. Also, opposition was expected from competing hospitals and physicians not

44

on the medical staffs of the three hospitals; accordingly, plans were made to deal with them.

Following the decision to establish a PPO, the author was assigned the task of taking the idea from conception to operation, and was charged with the responsibility of selecting the type of PPO and its organizational structure. Preliminary work included information gathering by means of an extensive literature review, participation in a symposium on PPOs, and on-site visits at two operational PPOs.

Reactions from the medical community varied. The state's largest organization of physicians viewed PPOs with skepticism because of the potential of this alternative delivery system to reduce income by forcing them to accept discounts for care; this organization opposed PPOs and discouraged members from participating on physician panels. Administrators of teaching hospitals expressed reservations about PPOs because the intense pressure to reduce costs affected the quality of education; moreover, they feared that PPOs would lure paying patients away from their facility and leave them with only indigent patients.

In contrast to the response of physicians and administrators, registered nurses seemed to view the establishment of PPOs as an opportunity to expand their role in medicine. The R.N.s felt that the costs of care could be reduced if they were allowed to take a more active role in patient diagnosis and treatment.

Administrative Decision

Early in our deliberation, the author and his colleagues discussed the wisdom of proceeding without the experience of our large competitors. We realized, however, that if we were not first into the market, our entry would be hampered by our lack of size; consequently, we began a search for available PPO plans.

We undertook an analysis of the market to determine the characteristics of our potential customer base, and also the type of PPO ownership structure that would provide the best potential for attracting physicians and patients to our facilities. Certain organizational arrangements which could result in anti-trust legal problems were identified and taken into account in our selection of a structure. While specific regulating mechanisms had not yet been formulated and possible legal entanglements still existed, management was convinced that the basic PPO premise of cost reduction through increased patient base would prove itself over the long term.

An agreement was reached with a preferred provider organization operating in another state to purchase all necessary forms, which included contracts, and computer software for claims processing and utilization review. Additionally, a prearranged fee was negotiated for consulting services, including speaking engagements, to assist with physician enrollments.

The organization of physicians proved a somewhat more difficult obstacle than was anticipated, because the malpractice carrier had determined (mistakenly) a clause in the physician agreement to be a "hold harmless" clause, which might interfere with coverage should the physician participate in the HMO. However, since the agreement was in use in other states, and had been found to be acceptable by physician groups and attorneys, the state's malpractice carrier acceded to the coverage. With removal of this barrier, physicians, dentists, and other health care professionals began to sign participation agreements and the PPO began to take shape.

A somewhat unique governing arrangement was established in order to avoid the potential problem of price-fixing--the negotiation of compensation rates by physician and payor. This situation was avoided by having an employee of the PPO negotiate with the payor for physicians' fee schedules or percentage discounts from normal and customary schedules. Once a discount is agreed upon for a particular group, the individual physician is given the option of participation.

This type of arrangement allows physicians and other PPO providers to be selective in their participation, and also removes them completely from any part of the negotiation process; many physicians expressed their approval of an arrangement in which they could participate in the PPO without having to become involved in every contract signed by the PPO. This has assisted in recruiting and retaining physicians.

The board of directors of the PPO is responsible for utilization review, physician discipline, and acceptance of additional physician members within the PPO. This governing body serves at the pleasure of the corporate board, which is appointed by the stockholders of the parent corporation. The governance of the PPO has worked well, with no problems resulting in physician discipline.

Results

Since the PPO was established, the number of admissions to Unity Care has increased by some 6.6 percent; the incremental increase in admissions would not have occurred without the aggressive actions that were taken. The establishment of the PPO has heightened interest in this type of alternative delivery system, and has provided a vehicle for contact with physicians who are not members of the medical staff. We believe that a successful track record will serve as an excellent recruitment tool for the PPO. A number of physicians who were members of the medical staff and had been utilizing other facilities have increased their utilization of our facilities following the establishment of the PPO. While it is difficult to determine why our larger competitors failed to enter the PPO market in our area, we suspect that our early entry into the market caused them to discount their probability of success.

Inasmuch as the PPO concept was completely new to our area--the nearest operational PPO is some 300 miles away--an informational marketing system was initiated in order to promote it with employers, physicians, and the public. Contact with all employers in the county with six or more employees was made through a direct mail campaign, which was followed by presentations to the local Personnel Director's Organization. Those businesses with corporate headquarters in distant cities, whose health benefit programs are determined at the corporate level, were also contacted.

Physician skepticism was reduced by means of informational visits that explained the method utilized to determine fees and percentage discounts. Additionally, each physician received a copy of the individual contract participation agreement, which allowed him/her to agree or decline to participate in each contract. Further, it was pointed out that there would also be a contract that would allow the physician to realize his customary fee. Physician acceptance of the fee arrangement was excellent, and many asserted that without such an agreement they would not participate in the PPO.

A thirty-second television promotional spot was produced, which outlined the problems associated with cost increases in health care in recent years and encouraged the viewer to contact the PPO for literature and/or a presentation. A print ad was produced and placed in the Sunday newspaper outlining the benefits of the PPO and suggesting that cost savings of 22 to 40 percent could be realized in certain cases. Nearly 9,000 participants were enrolled within four months of the program's beginning. Possibly, an increase in insurance rates will cause an increase in the number of contracts in the future.

Although we had not anticipated many of the problems we encountered in establishing the first PPO in a very conservative market, we feel vindicated by the results: our method has the potential to attract patients to a particular facility and to a particular group of physicians. Because of recent governmental decisions to expand the participation of Medicare recipients in competitive medical programs, including HMOs, a decision was reached to apply our newly acquired knowledge concerning the operation of a PPO to the development of a health maintenance organization.

Organization Information

Faith Hospital is a 451 bed facility, with a medical staff of 639, representing 21 specialties. Hope Medical Center is a 483 bed facility with a 550 member medical staff serving 20 specialties. Both hospital and medical center are not-for-profit community facilities governed by the nine-member board of a religious order. Both are tertiary teaching institutions serving as major referral hospitals for the state, and are situated in a metropolitan area of over one million people.

Gist of the Problem

This report describes the complications involved in acquiring an alternative delivery system in a metropolitan area market. It discusses those products that currently exist in the market, and it examines the options for development of a preferred provider organization.

Description of the Problem

Faith Hospital and Hope Medical Center, in cooperation with a separately incorporated independent practice association of physicians, had developed a health maintenance organization. Despite the success of the HMO, the volatility of the health care market suggested that other health financing mechanisms would be required in order to satisfy employers, insurers, and purchasers who had chosen not to commit to an HMO plan, but who demonstrated interest in an alternative delivery system to control health care costs and provide access to quality services. For this reason, development of a preferred provider organization was suggested.

The area health care market was flooded with various insurance and payment models which represented no fewer than nine major competing plans and covered 40 percent of the market. Although the hospital and medical center had entered the ADS market, it was not clear what financing mechanisms (i.e., HMO, PPO, fee-for-service) would be most successful in the long run. This being the case, a PPO model was considered in order to respond to possible changes in market demands.

At the outset, the case writer and his colleagues were faced with problems. For example, we had to determine the most advantageous type of ownership, either solo or joint; shared ownership, we knew, would enhance the availability of necessary capital and diminish the political risk, but it would also dilute control. In addition, we believed that the management and marketing of the PPO through our HMO would only serve to confuse the public. We also knew that a number of insurance companies were moving to develop a "triple option" indemnity, PPO, HMO portfolio.

In order to address these problems, a task force was appointed with representatives from each institution and the HMO. The mission of this task force was to investigate options, to propose a strategy, and to recommend steps necessary to develop an appropriate PPO model for this market.

Administrative Decision

In arriving at a decision, the task force evaluated a number of elements:

1) Market: An entire range of different market combinations may exist, and it was imperative that we decide which market we intended to compete in.

2) Products: It was also important to identify the major characteristics of a successful health care financing/cost-containment product. Among the alternative products were (a) the fully-insured plans, including Blue Cross/Blue Shield and commercial indemnity plans; (b) minimum premium arrangements, which include resources managed by the buyer and combine the features of self-funding with stop-loss protection from the insurer; (c) fully self-funded plans, which provide the opportunity to unbundle benefits and offer a great deal of flexibility; and (d) the HMO model, which typically maximizes the control features of capitation and provider access in return for maximum cost control and premium savings for the self-funded employer.

3) Organization: Any PPO operation requires a policy making function, which involves a board for execution of specific objectives and operational components of the PPO.

4) Services: The hospital component needs to be capable of quality assurance, administrative support (finances, marketing, contract management), and a full range of health care services.

5) Physicians: Since this PPO venture was a joint enterprise with physicians, it was important to have the physicians involved in policy making functions. The physician organization could be represented in a number of ways, including (a) the medical staff organization of each hospital; (b) a new independent practice association established through interested members of the medical staff; and (c) the existing independent practice association formed by the physicians of the hospital and the medical center to implement the HMO. The physicians would be able to (a) select leadership; (b)

develop a physician organization; (c) determine criteria for physician selection; (d) establish performance standards, utilization review, and quality assurance; and (e) set professional service fees.

6) Data Processing: The PPO function requires a database for management control, population analysis, market penetration, utilization review, routine financial statements, individual provider reports, and claims. It is important that this base be integrated into the premium development process and the claims cost projections if the underwriting entity is to be self-insured. Options for data processing include (a) delegation of responsibility to the existing hospital staff; (b) purchase of service through a third party administrator; and (c) development of the PPO's own data processing capability.

7) Utilization Review/Quality Assurance: Among the system's required components are (a) ambulatory care--including the primary care component, the doctor's office; (b) detailed analysis of practice patterns and development of physician profiles; (c) an inpatient component that includes pre-admission certification, concurrent review, ancillary service review, and surgical review. This need can be met in a number of ways, including support secured from the hospital for certain utilization and question-answer review functions, or purchased through an outside organization.

8) Benefit Design: Design of the benefit package is largely determined by the employer and/or their representative insurance carrier. Many buyers modify existing insurance plans by shifting costs to employees and providers. It is essential that the PPO be differentiated from the HMO and existing indemnity plans.

9) Reimbursement Methodologies: As multiple PPO arrangements are secured, policies on discounting must be prepared. These include a straight discount from established fee schedules, floating discounts based on volume, all-inclusive per diems, negotiated per diems for specific services, diagnostic related groups, and modified DRG systems for physicians and hospitals with shared savings generated among the hospital, participating physician, and buyer.

10) Marketing: It is important to recognize that a PPO is not marketed like an HMO. Access to the PPO is through the employer health benefits plan, which implies a need to work closely with the employer in benefit design--the PPO is an option to those employees who have chosen not to be in an HMO.

The task force carefully examined the available strategies for implementation of the PPO concept:

1) Establish a separate, corporate entity for PPO activities. This corporation would contract with the buyer and subcontract separately with the hospitals for benefit design, administrative services, and provider services (including the physician component to provide utilization review).

2) A second option is to take an equity position in an existing PPO organization. This approach takes advantage of existing resources, and avoids reinventing the wheel, while providing an expedient position for the hospitals in marketing an established PPO. Moreover, it separates the buyer from the provider through a broker--which is considered by some to be important.

3) A third alternative is to joint venture with a prominent insurance company and the IPA to develop a competitive, limited provider indemnity health plan based on fee-for-service practice. Such a relationship would assist in underwriting and marketing the product in this area.

4) Finally, an organization could be established through the existing hospital staff that represents both operations and finance. Each preferred provider opportunity would be evaluated by the project team. Resources to provide utilization review, contracting of fee schedule for hospitals and physicians, and marketing and benefit design would be arranged through existing hospital or affiliated organization services.

It should be remembered that these are just several of various structures that can be combined to meet both short and long-term objectives. In order to evaluate the alternatives, the task force developed criteria important to organizational success. They include: (1) implementation; (2) flexibility; (3) control; (4) product strength; (5) accountability; (6) viability; (7) physician compatibility; (8) market potential; and (9) cost.

Interviews were conducted with the leadership of the four PPO providers, after which the task force determined that the hospital and medical center should take controlling equity position in an existing PPO in order to provide both resource commitment and policy direction. This approach would offer the advantages of control, limited risk, flexibility for future changes, and the know-how of an existing business.

Results

Following the report of the task force, action was taken to acquire the local PPO. The acquisition recommendation was accepted by administrators of Faith Hospital and Hope Medical Center within one month of the expiration of the task force's term. Acquisition provided both institutions with the opportunity to move quickly on preferred provider and limited contracting opportunities. The initiatives we exercised in marketing our hospitals and in utilizing the increased visibility of the preferred provider organization, have had favorable results--demonstrated by the acquisition of 15 new clients, including a regional union health trust.

The purchase arrangement included a provision whereby the purchase value of the acquired firm will be significantly tied to future success. That is, at the outset the hospitals provided capital representing approximately one-half of the estimated business value, and in three years will provide the second half of the agreed to price--after demonstrated success.

III. Introduction to Alternatives to Inpatient Care: Diversification Activities

In each of the following cases, the author identifies a changing health care environment in which fewer patients and reduced revenues create a need for expanded service lines to ensure financial viability. In several of these cases, a further incentive is the pressing imperative of an expanding health care mission. The first two cases deal with the development by a hospital of a freestanding ambulatory care center; cases three and four present the establishment of home care capabilities by a health organization; the last two cases show the health care mission extended to embrace chemical dependency and hospice programs.

A. Freestanding Clinics

"Justification and Development of a Freestanding Ambulatory Care Center" can, perhaps, serve as a representative case for a hospital seeking new revenue sources through the development of a new health service. After determining the need for diversification and then completing market and statistical analyses, the hospital management resolves to develop a freestanding ambulatory care facility. The feasibility study shows the advantages offered by such a service: (1) the opportunity to develop new health programs, (2) improved access to care for consumers, and (3) lower cost for care. Also considered are the American Hospital Association's criteria for the establishment of an ambulatory care service, the specific identity of the service, and the enlistment of physician support. Following a year of research, the developmental phase is initiated with the submission of a set of recommendations to the hospital board of trustees. A further note of interest here is the mention of "image enhancement" in connection with the development of an ambulatory care facility- a hospital that reaches out into the community with a new low-cost program is likely to enhance its public profile and be viewed as a progressive institution.

"A Hospital System's Approach to Freestanding Emergency Clinics" resembles the previous case in its preliminary search for new revenue sources, and in the careful market study it carries out as part of the feasibility phase. This case is distinct from the others, however, in that it is essentially a report on an endeavor that fails:the minor emergency clinic sponsored by the multihospital system ultimately closes due to a combination of reasons. Yet the story of a failure can be as instructive as one of success if the writer makes some attempt to understand the reasons for the failure--as this one does. Notable aspects of this case are the careful deliberation shown by the representatives of Galen Health Care in their approach to the development of the minor emergency clinics, and the design of the ownership structure of the clinics. The multihospital system creates a subsidiary corporation which develops clinic sites, then under-

53

takes to lease them to physicians; the advantages of this arrangement are discussed and problems analyzed. A partnership is formed with a physician who leases two clinic facilities from the corporation with the understanding that referrals are to go to Galen Health Care. The reason for the closing of the clinics, the physician's failure to make his rent payments, is a consequence of a number of conditions: poor business practices on the part of the physician, lack of initial advertising, incorrect marketing information regarding referrals, and unexpected competition from other clinics.

Justification and Development of a Freestanding Ambulatory Care Center

Organization Information

Mercy Hospital is one of 22 general acute health facilities in a major metropolitan area of the southern United States. Although this medical facility has only 275 acute care beds, its services and facilities are more in line with those of a much larger medical center. It is a not-for-profit hospital under the supervision of a religious order of Sisters, who own and operate hospitals throughout the U.S. The corporate body is comprised of Sisters, who delegate the policy making to a board of trustees.

Over the years, Mercy Hospital has maintained the second best occupancy rate in the metropolitan area, and in recent years it has been noted for its creative approach to health care delivery in a very competitive market. In addition, it has a reputation for being the leading cancer treatment center in the metropolitan area. Although small by metropolitan standards, this facility is a full-service medical center that is able to be competitive with major medical centers in the area.

Gist of the Problem

Like many health care facilities, Mercy Hospital was interested in developing new revenue sources by means of new programs and services. In order to maintain and increase its market share and to provide needed health services at a location other than the hospital complex, the hospital management had to decide on a suitable "vehicle."

Description of the Problem

In a rapidly changing health care environment, the primary concern of many hospitals is simply survival. The goal of Mercy was not only to survive but to prosper, and we knew that in order to do so we had to develop new revenue sources utilizing new programs and services. An analysis of population trends in the primary and secondary service areas of the hospital was conducted utilizing U.S. Department of Commerce census data. The study revealed that during the period 1970 to 1980, the total population in the primary service area decreased by 8.9 percent, and by 1985 a further decrease of 1.9 percent had occurred. These figures reflected a need for the hospital to make a greater effort to maintain its share of the market.

After in-depth study of the market and statistical analysis, we decided to pursue economic growth by means of a comprehensive program for a freestanding ambulatory care facility. Ambulatory care was defined as a facility that provides outpatient surgery, urgent and/or emergency care, outpatient rehabilitative services, preventive health and fitness, and diagnostic and therapeutic services. An ambulatory care facility would allow the hospital to maintain market share in its service area by:

1)   increasing community awareness of the hospital's services;

2)   providing new health care programs that are ambulatory based;

3)   improving the access to health care in the service area;

4)   and providing health care at a lower cost to the patient.

Mercy's need to increase its share of the primary market area was affected by the change in demand for medical services in the metropolitan area over the past decade. Much of the demand had centered on the need for emergency services. It was estimated that 20 percent of emergency room visits involved life threatening situations, while the remaining 80 percent were primary care visits. We therefore concluded that the development of an ambulatory care facility would allow the hospital to meet the need for primary care services that are accessible, convenient, and cost effective.

A freestanding ambulatory care facility can provide various services, but such services are dependent on the hospital's need, the market need, and the purpose of the facility. We determined that a freestanding facility for emergency care in an area not currently served by a hospital or ambulatory care center would increase our inpatient market share through a greater number of admissions. Statistics showed that approximately 2-6 percent of patients seen in emergency care centers become inpatient admissions to a hospital.

Another advantage was a charge to the patient considerably less than that incurred in the hospital's emergency room, owing to a lower overhead; in an ambulatory care facility, minor emergencies tend to be the rule, whereas a hospital emergency room tends to prepare for major acute emergency problems. Disadvantages included a negative impact on the utilization of the hospital's emergency department in the first year. According to studies, however, in the second and subsequent years the utilization of the hospital's emergency department returns to prior levels. We determined that the potential for increased admissions would be far greater in a freestanding ambulatory facility, oriented to minor emergencies, than in an in-hospital facility.

According to experts in the field of ambulatory care, the location of an ambulatory care facility is of critical importance. The market analysis showed that there were three viable location alternatives: (1) the hospital's primary service area, (2) the hospital's secondary service zone, and (3) the central business district. In reviewing selected statistics relating to discharges from hospitals in our metropolitan area, we determined that our hospital was one of the dominant private hospitals in its primary service area. Even so, according to a study done for Mercy Hospital, patients living in the primary service area preferred two other hospitals to our facility. The report went on to say that since there were relatively small differences between our hospital and the others, we ought to attempt to capture customers by means of a freestanding emergency center. The study also suggested that such a facility in the primary service area would help us to maintain and increase market share. Here was an opportunity to present our hospital as a progressive institution that reaches out into the community to make itself more responsive to the needs of the citizens.

In searching for a specific location, we weighed the American Hospital Association's criteria for the establishment of an ambulatory care center. Among those elements are: (a) high traffic count (25,000 per day); (b) left turn from main road; (c) high visibility; (d) noticeable signs; (e) ample parking; and (f) front on main road.

Another major problem to be considered was physician support. Once the site had been selected, the physicians who would be most directly affected by the establishment of a center had to be identified, and apprised of the center's purpose and potential impact. The same applied to the medical staff, who we felt ought to be in support of what the hospital was attempting to achieve.

The last major problem was consideration of cost. For a freestanding center to be successful, it must offer fast service at a price that is less than that of a hospital emergency room. In order to achieve that, the center must have as much flexibility as possible so that it is able to compete effectively for those patients who are using other health providers. We knew that we had to provide a high quality, attractive product at the lowest possible price.

Administrative Decision

After in-depth research over a period of 12 months, the staff recommended the following to the board of trustees:

1)   The hospital should develop a freestanding ambulatory care center in its primary service area in order to maintain and increase its portion of the health care market in the metropolitan area. Such a center would enhance the image of the hospital as a progressive, need-oriented institution.

2)   The center should provide minor emergency care and facilities for consumer education in that part of the city.

3)   The location should be in close proximity to the city-county line, preferably on the county side.

4)   Medical staff already in favor of the proposal should be asked to help sell the program to their physician colleagues.

Results

Two years have passed and our freestanding ambulatory care center is the largest and most comprehensive facility of its kind in the metropolitan area. The new facility has already increased the public's awareness of Mercy Hospital, and it is in one of the most visible locations in the county. Besides having eight treatment rooms, a small laboratory and general diagnostic x-ray facilities, the center provides a community education program for over 200 persons. The facility is open 16 hours a day, seven days a week. It is staffed with a medical doctor who is on the medical staff of the hospital, an R.N., a technician, and a receptionist. All were hired on the basis of ability and skills, with a strong emphasis on selecting those who had an outgoing, pleasant personality. The initial community response and acceptance have been overwhelming. The visibility of Mercy Hospital's name is now greater than ever and, more important, a need for this particular type of health care is being met. In view of current trends and projections, we anticipate a profit within 12 months time.

A Hospital System's Approach to Freestanding Emergency Clinics

Organization Information

Galen Health Care is a 1350 bed not-for-profit multihospital system, headquartered in a large industrial city. The system consists of two large flagship hospitals in the city, and three smaller leased or owned facilities within a 100-mile radius. The organization is sponsored by a local religious association which appoints its 25 member governing board. The city has a population of approximately 800,000, and is served by 18 general and five specialty hospitals, several of which serve the region as major referral centers and provide a wide variety of tertiary care services.

Galen Health Care's Corporate Services Division is charged with the responsibility of investigating alternative delivery systems which can be integrated into the system's health care network. The Vice President for Shared Services (the casewriter) was asked to explore the health care phenomenon known as minor emergency clinics.

Gist of the Problem

Galen Health Care was faced with declining utilization of emergency room facilities at its flagship hospitals as a result of the development of minor emergency clinics by health care providers and outside investors. The challenge confronting the corporate division was developing some means to protect against the loss of business.

Description of the Problem

The casewriter was given the responsibility of investigating the local proliferation of minor emergency clinics, which were part of a national chain. While the majority of the clinics were owned and operated by private physicians, for-profit hospital management corporations were becoming increasingly interested in the development of such facilities. Not-for-profit hospitals had an interest in the clinics as well, but had lagged behind the others in pursuing that interest.

We felt that the development of minor emergency clinics would have substantial ramifications for hospitals. For one thing, the clinics contributed directly to a reduction in the number of private pay patients treated in hospital emergency rooms, which led to a decrease in total revenue. In view of the planned development of minor emergency clinics throughout the city, we felt that this trend toward lower emergency room utilization would be exacerbated. Management decided to encourage the development of minor emergency clinics by interested physicians in the hope of developing referrals to increase emergency room utilization and hospital inpatient admissions.

Administrative Decision

Galen Heath Care formed a proprietary subsidiary corporation for the purpose of subleasing improved store-front office space for the operation of the clinics. Although the leasing arrangement did not require the referral of patients to either of the flagship hospitals, referrals were anticipated nonetheless.

The casewriter conducted a review of the literature on minor emergency clinics, then undertook a site visit to a neighboring city to inspect this type of alternative delivery system. Such clinics provide for the treatment of acute, episodic medical problems of a minor nature. Characteristically, they operate 12 to 16 hours a day, seven days a week, require payment when treatment is rendered, and do not accept Medicare or Medicaid. Generally, these clinics do not schedule appointments and do not attempt to provide continuity of care for the patient. This system of treatment focuses on prompt attention to walk-in patients.

Discussions between the casewriter and officers of Galen centered on the hours of operation, staffing requirements, rate schedules, the scope of services rendered, the continuity of care issue, payment policies, routine operating costs, and the role and expense of advertising in the development of clinics. It was decided that a marketing study should be undertaken to determine the acceptability of minor emergency clinics in the marketplace. When the operating assumptions were agreed upon, the development of pro formas for the clinics was undertaken.

The author met with the president of the Emergency Room Physicians Group to respond to the interest of this group in developing industrial clinics, and also to reduce potential medical staff conflicts. The president expressed some interest in negotiating with the multihospital system to develop minor emergency clinics in the city. It was his perception that such clinics provided a feeder system of patients to medical staff specialists.

As the initial pro formas were being developed, the marketing survey results were finalized: they indicated a high level acceptance of the minor emergency clinic concept. An analysis of the survey showed that this high level of acceptance was a result of both the clinic's perceived ability to provide faster care at a lower cost than the hospital emergency room, and also its more personal treatment.

A second market study was conducted to locate sites for the potential clinics. The ensuing analysis examined population density, income level, and the commercial/industrial mix of the area. From this study, three locations were identified. (At the time of the study, there were no urgent care facilities in the areas identified.) The site analyses resulted in utilization projections for the clinics which were then used in the development of pro formas. These projections indicated a positive cash flow within four months, with the clinics' breaking even within 12 months of their opening.

A major consideration in this process was the ownership model under which the clinics would be developed. The basic alternatives included ownership of the clinics by Galen, physician ownership of the clinics, and a partnership arrangement between the physicians and Galen.

Closely related to the issue of ownership was the question of corporate structure. Early in the discussion of minor emergency clinics, consideration was given to establishing a separate proprietary corporation to handle the development of the clinics. By this means, certificate of need approval could be avoided, and a new corporation could take advantage of tax shields which could not be used by Galen Health Care. Controlling interest in the new corporation, however, would be maintained by the multihospital system.

Once the pro formas were completed, and the marketing department had located potential sites for the clinics, the author met with the Management Executive Committee to present his proposal. We proposed a separate corporation, which in turn would establish a partnership with a physician or physician group to develop and promote minor emergency clinics within the areas identified by the market study. The subsidiary would negotiate a contract with the physicians to provide medical services, and would make available to them the purchase of up to 49 percent of the stock in the company. This would allow for participation and profits, distributed as dividends, and create incentive for the physicians to promote the success of the clinics. The board of the new corporation would be appointed by Galen as majority stockholder.

The possibility of establishing a partnership with the Emergency Room Physician Group was not ruled out, although it was noted that the services of that group had been acquired for the Primary Care Centers of Galen Health Care. It was decided that another physician group should be contacted regarding the development of the minor emergency clinics, rather than have the emergency rooms, primary care clinics, and minor emergency clinics all dependent upon the services of one group of physicians.

The administrators of the flagship hospitals were concerned that the members of the medical staffs would see the development of the clinics as competition. Although the clinics would provide referrals to staff specialists, there existed the potential for drawing patients away from both internists and family practitioners. There was also some concern that by selling stock to the physicians involved, Galen would be viewed as providing

61

preferential treatment to particular physicians. Based on these concerns, the matter was tabled for future discussion.

Other physicians in the community showed considerable interest in minor emergency clinics; construction was begun on several, and announcements of plans for future clinics were made. The author was contacted by a physician who announced that he was opening a minor emergency clinic in the city. The physician expressed an interest in referring patients to both of the flagship hospitals of the multihospital system, because of the reputation for quality at both facilities. The author determined that the physician would be interested in establishing a formal relationship with Galen if it were possible for him to open more than one clinic.

An agreement between the physician and the subsidiary corporation of the hospital was negotiated; it provided the physician with a line of credit to establish two minor emergency clinics, and to sublease the store-front office space which had been equipped for use as a clinic. The clinic business would belong to the physician and would be his sole responsibility.

In return, the physician agreed to a lease-plus arrangement whereby he paid to the subsidiary corporation a base rental rate plus five percent of the gross revenues. The base rate provided for the leasing of the store-front office space by the subsidiary corporation, and the amortization of the remodeling expenses and equipment costs to furnish the clinic. The line of credit available to the physician was repayable within the first 12 months without interest, or at a rate of eight percent on the unpaid balance after 12 months.

Based on the feasibility study conducted by the marketing department, and the operational input received from the physician, a pro forma was developed. A positive cash flow was expected within the first four months, and the clinics were expected to break even within the first year of operation. With the approval of the medical staff leadership, and the hospital administrators of the flagship hospitals, the subsidiary was incorporated and the agreement between the physician and the subsidiary was signed.

Results

Two clinics subleased from the subsidiary corporation were opened within the same year. Neither saw the number of patients anticipated, owing in part to the lack of initial promotion. Both the original site visit and the review of literature revealed the need for substantial advertising just prior to and following the opening of the clinics. Advertising expenditures were included in the pro forma estimates and were taken into consideration when the line of credit was negotiated. But promotion was piecemeal, at best.

The physician depended on office personnel at each clinic to collect fees from patients at the time of the visit. This was not done effectively, and the result was a higher than normal accounts receivable for each clinic. The billing system that the physician had purchased from a commercial firm charged for each patient seen, including those who had paid in full at the time of the visit. Old acounts were not reviewed by the physician until 120 days after the patient's initial visit. Since the probability of successful collection efforts was less than 50 percent after 90 days, the probability of collecting after 120 days was even less. Clearly, the physician-owner of the minor emergency clinics was not employing good business practice; moreover, he resisted pressure to hire a business manager to bring order to his operations.

A collection system that was ineffective and overpriced, and a lack of management information characterized the operation of the facilities. Subsequently, the physician fell behind in his lease payments to the subsidiary corporation, and eventually, he was evicted under the terms of his lease.

The loss of referrals was minimal, since only a small number of patients seen in the clinic were without a personal physician. The majority of patients visiting the clinics did so as a stop-gap measure until they could see their own physician. This result was inconsistent with the original marketing information, which had indicated that a large percentage of the clinics' potential users did not have a regular physician. We had hoped that this portion of the consumer public would utilize the minor emergency clinics as a matter of convenience and could then be referred to either flagship hospital as needed.

The marketing department discovered that several episodic care facilities had been established in the designated areas to compete with the minor emergency clinics. As the competition increased, demand for services at the clinics decreased. Without tight fiscal controls, or adequate management information, the clinics could not be managed properly. Ultimately this led to the termination of the lease by the subsidiary corporation.

To salvage the investment in the clinics, the subsidiary sub-leased the clinics to other physicians for the remainder of the original lease agreements. These leases were negotiated to allow for the subsidiary corporation to recoup some of its expenses. The decision was made not to exercise the option to renew the leases on the clinic space upon expiration of the initial term of the lease.

B. Home Care

"Home Care Diversification: Developing a Strategic Plan" presents a detailed, step-by-step approach to diversification. As with the other cases, this begins with the statement of a familiar problem: reduced hospital revenues and a consequent need to diversify in order to hold and/or enhance market share. A further problem is how to "develop a strategic plan for diversification, without the benefit of market data, for businesses in which we had no experience and in a marketplace which was very competitive and constantly changing." Of particular interest in this case report is the feasibility study. The management team completes extensive internal and external assessments in which elements that bear on the diversification are carefully examined. Relevant aspects include existing home care referral patterns, availability of resources, and the amount and severity of competition in the market. Following this analysis, a strategic plan is drawn up.

The blueprint that results from this analysis recommends diversification into three home care related businesses (extensions of certified home health agency services), risk reduction by means of joint ventures, and the solicitation of proposals from firms in each business. According to the author, three criteria by which the success of a strategic plan is judged are: (1) the ability to bear the rigors of negotiation with experienced partners; (2) flexibility (room for modification); and (3) internal acceptance of the plan. Another feature of note here--one similar to that of an earlier case--is the overriding concern with public image. "A major concern for the board and management team was to keep the diversification efforts in line with the hospital's mission and current operations."

"Establishment of a Home Care Department Through Collaborative Efforts with a Sister Hospital," like the previous case, presents the situation of a hospital interested in the enhancement of market share as well as public image. The home care program is intended to allow the hospital to strengthen competitive position in a changing market, and also to extend its health care mission by providing continuity of care following discharge from the hospital. In the feasibility study, the options of a solo in-house and a shared contracted program are examined; the advantages and disadvantages are identified and weighed. Like other ventures in diversification, this one considers the merits of a cooperative venture with an existing organization; the benefits of this arrangement include the reduction of financial risk and start-up time, and the availability of resources and management expertise. In spite of the positive results of the collaborative effort, certain problems remain: sharing of revenues with the sister hospital, dilution of administrative authority, and logistical difficulties created by the distance between the administrative staff at the two hospitals.

Home Care Diversification: Developing a Strategic Plan

Organization Information

St. Joseph Hospital is a 415 bed Catholic facility under the auspices of the regional diocese, and is governed with considerable independence by its own board of trustees. The bishop of the diocese serves as chairman, ex-officio of the board.

St. Joseph has serviced a suburban area outside New York City for 26 years. There are 12 towns in the hospital's primary service area, and 11 towns in its secondary service area. The population base in this area is approximately 500,000 but the density is considered moderate because of the large geographical area.

Recently, St. Joseph commenced operation of a certified home health care agency which provides a full range of home health care services, including nursing, social work, home health aides, and all therapies. The home health care agency is managed as a division of the hospital, and is licensed by the state and certified by Medicare.

Gist of the Problem

In a changing reimbursement environment, St. Joseph Hospital began to explore alternative means for generating additional sources of revenue. Diversification into home health care related businesses was a logical choice, but it was unclear which of these businesses the hospital should pursue and what the competition would be. A major concern of diversification was how to maximize market share without (1) making a major dollar investment; (2) compromising the quality of care provided; and (3) incurring too much financial risk. A top management team assessed both the internal and external environments, met with firms anxious to form joint ventures, obtained legal and financial advice from consultants, and developed a strategic plan for diversification which they tested and fine-tuned during initial joint venture negotiations.

Description of the Problem

Four years ago the St. Joseph board of trustees began to analyze the challenges facing hospitals, as well as the various strategic approaches necessary to assure the institution's continued financial viability. Recently, a corporate holding company was established for the hospital. It was understood that as future businesses were developed, they would be organized as separate subsidiaries of the holding company; it was then left to management to develop an approach to diversification, to select the business, and to formulate appropriate plans. A major concern for the board and management was to keep the diversification efforts in line with

65

the hospital's mission and current operations. Although the board recognized the pressing need to explore new and diverse opportunities, it nevertheless took a conservative approach to any new venture, as it was keenly interested in maintaining St. Joseph's excellent public image.

The author spent part of two years developing and implementing St. Joseph's certified home health agency (CHHA), which included nursing care. The nursing service was significant in that most hospital-based agencies contracted for nursing services, which meant a loss of control over the coordination of care and products provided. Two years ago the author began an informal assessment of diversification opportunities in the home care field. In addition to the certified services provided by CHHAs, three other major categories of businesses were (1) durable medical equipment (DME); (2) infusion therapies such as Total Parenteral Nutrition (TNP) chemotherapy, and IV antibiotics which were collectively known as the "high tech" services; and (3) routine home care services such as those provided by CHHAs, but more directed toward the self-paying and commercially-insured patient. (Examples are around-the-clock nursing and home health aide or homemaker services.)

Diversifying into these areas appeared reasonable because (1) they represented an extension of our own CHHA's services; (2) they were in keeping with the mission of St. Joseph; (3) they fit in with the hospital's provider network which included a nursing home, a chronic dialysis center, and a proposed long-term home health care program; and (4) these services were becoming lucrative markets. We knew that the hospital's provider network was a source of consumers and direct referrals, and also that our CHAA was the only hospital-based agency in our region competitively positioned to coordinate all aspects of home care. Consequently, we concluded that we could achieve an advantage in the home care marketplace.

The author assumed leadership of an administrative team that was charged with developing a strategic plan for home care diversification. We were confronted by a rapidly changing and very competitive home care market with little reliable data on which to build projections. Although few hospitals were positioned to compete with us, a large number of proprietary firms were vying for the home care markets; large national firms were moving rapidly to buy out smaller businesses. Clearly, a major "shake out" of the industry was underway.

In addition, an anticipated change in state regulations was about to permit proprietary agencies to become certified for the first time, thereby adding competition in the area of Medicare-certified services. Changes were also taking place in Medicare regulations pertaining to DME and high-tech services, and these changes were beginning to "squeeze" these once quite profitable businesses. In short, St. Joseph faced a formidable task in developing a strategic plan for diversifying further into home care services.

Administrative Decision

As noted, there was no home care market data readily available for our region, and we knew our hospital could not afford a costly market survey to gather this type of information. Our administrative team determined that we would have to gather this data ourselves. For the next seven months we tapped every source of home care information we could think of. Through extensive reading and personal contacts, we were able to assess the three major categories of business (DME, high-tech, and routine home care) and the various strategies used to diversify into them. We met with a large number of proprietary firms anxious to establish joint ventures with us, and we visited hospitals that had already implemented such new businesses. We completed formal and informal surveys of our internal and external environment and sought legal and financial advice to fine tune our thinking. Finally, we did a lot of pure brainstorming about where institutional and non-institutional health care was heading, and how we might position ourselves to take advantage of it.

We concluded that St.Joseph should diversify into all three major home care areas open to us, and that we should do so at once. Increasing competition and changing regulations would soon make entry into these marketplaces much more difficult. We decided against developing our own internal expertise, and resolved instead to form three joint ventures concurrently, all of which would be responsible to a for-profit subsidiary of St. Joseph's parent corporation. Finally, through negotiations with potential joint venture partners, we refined our strategic plan to mix and match the capital and time requirements of each venture so as to achieve a workable method for diversifying into all three areas.

In the early phases of our work, our administrative team analyzed the three major business areas. "High tech" services was viewed as a low-volume, high-profit-margin business which tended to be dominated by a handful of large pharmaceutical companies. Recent Medicare changes had cut into high tech's profit margin, but we anticipated that DRGs would promote greater home care demand for IV antibiotics and chemotherapy. DME was a high volume business whose mixed profit margins were a result of changing Medicare regulations. The large volume generated equally large revenues, and made this an attractive market for many competitors. Routine home care services had mixed volumes and profit margins and attracted a very large number of competitors. We projected that volume would only increase with DRGs and an aging population, however, and we ascertained that no firm had a dominant share of our region's marketplace. Four strategic options were identified as means for participating in these business areas:

1)   making referrals only;

2)   forming a joint venture with exchange of services only;

3)   forming a joint venture through a partnership or new
       corporation;

4)   developing new businesses independently.

"Making referrals only" represented the alternative requiring the least capital and time to set up, the least amount of risk, and the lowest financial return. Developing our own businesses independently represented the other extreme, and the two joint-venture opportunities represented compromises on cost, time, risk, and return.

The best option for each business was going to depend on how we viewed the internal and external environments. Having outlined our options, we began to conduct various formal and informal surveys, bringing in legal and financial consultants and applying our own sense of judgment and timing to the opportunities presented. Our internal assessment involved eight factors:

1)   the name and reputation of the hospital;

2)   existing organizational structure;

3)   internal attitudes toward profits;

4)   existing home care referral patterns;

5)   internal business/entrepreneur skills;

6)   existing business relationships;

7)   availability of resources;

8)   organizational climate.

To successfully compete, we had to ensure that our services or products were identified as different or better than those of our competitors. We already knew that St. Joseph Hospital had an excellent reputation, and a survey of over 500 home care clients indicated that our home care services were considered special as well. Consequently, we felt that our brand name had high and very positive visibility. We also knew that we had an organizational structure that would accommodate new subsidiaries.

We surveyed the hospital's discharge planners, home care coordinators, top home care referring physicians, and our nursing staff to identify any existing home care service referral patterns. Fortunately, none existed--this would have inhibited referrals to our own businesses.

Two important points need to be made with regard to referrals: (1) prior to St. Joseph's CHHA becoming operational, a public health nurse handled all home care discharge planning, thus preventing informal patterns from being established; (2) the CHHA's home care coordinators replaced this nurse, and began to support our ventures.

We determined that our internal business/entrepreneurial skills would be a major limiting factor. We were forced to contend with many internal "turf" and expertise issues. Some individuals within the hospital believed they had the expertise to develop and run these businesses, or they believed it was their responsibility to do so. Convincing them otherwise proved to be a very delicate operation. Also, our team had to exercise care in current business relationships with product or service vendors. Many of these were potential competitors to our new ventures. In our discussion they tended to overemphasize the competition in the marketplace and the importance of their own roles in home care. Ultimately, we identified two qualified existing vendors and included them as potential joint venturers.

Aside from entrepreneurial/management skills, three major resources were necessary to make our new venture a success: space, time, and money. We concluded that the new ventures would have to use off-site rented space, and would have to stand on their own operationally; they should not require more than $50-75,000, depending on projected rate of return. Finally, we assessed our organizational climate for elements such as quality, flexibility, and responsiveness.

The assessment of our external environment focused on four factors:

1) the legal issues of fraud and abuse in Medicare provisions and anti-trust regulations;

2) the amount and severity of competition in the markets;

3) the rate of success in comparable environments;

4) and timing.

In assessing these factors, we made use of outside legal and financial advice. We also found that a great deal of information could be gathered directly and indirectly from meeting with potential partners in joint ventures. Based on our attorney's advice, we concluded that our new ventures could avoid legal entanglements if patients were assured freedom of choice, and if the operations of our subsidiaries were kept separate and distinct from St. Joseph's.

Assessing the competition was much more difficult. We identified the number of firms in the market through a survey of the yellow pages. Many of the financial projections we developed were based on information provided through joint venture proposals, with additional insight and assistance from a home care financial consultant, and information obtained through published financial analysis of these markets. Our team felt that our provider network occupied such a unique niche in our region that we could succeed despite intensive competition. This attitude was reinforced when we examined the rate of success in comparable environments and talked with other successfully diversified hospitals.

The most difficult factor to assess objectively was timing. As noted, the home care marketplace was undergoing rapid and significant change and was not the place for hesitation or half-measures. Furthermore, no amount of quantitative analysis could identify the correct meshing of internal and external conditions vital for our success.

Despite all the previous decisions our team had made, the entire process came down to the collective judgment and intuition of our administrative group. We concluded that despite slowing growth rates and increased competition in these markets, home care would continue as a lucrative market, where the key to success would be in controlling referrals. Our internal environment and management team was well positioned for such an effort; if we did not act promptly we would lose an opportunity to be competitive. Because of our Hospital's unique situation, our chances for success were excellent.

The strategic plan we recommended contained three major provisions:

1) That the parent corporation form a for-profit subsidiary that would enter into contractual agreements with experienced firms; this was the preferred method for establishing the joint ventures, because such agreements would allow us to have access to needed expertise, and also because this option presented opportunities for generating revenues without major financial investment or major risk.

2) That the subsidiary enter into the three major home care types of businesses in the following sequence:

a) "hi-tech" services (infusion therapies) -- this was recommended first because of the high profit margin, the need to support hospice types of services, and the trend under DRGs to discharge patients sooner;

b) routine home care services (nursing, home health aids, etc.) -- given our certified agency's competitive position, we wanted to capitalize on that advantage and expand into the non-certified home care market and be in a position to support long-term home care programs as well;

c) durable medical equipment -- although probably the largest source of home care revenue, this is a more complicated business with higher capital requirements. Our team felt it would take longer to develop a joint venture.

3)   That proposals be solicited from four to six firms in each business area, to be narrowed down to one joint venture partner in each area. Given our lack of experience in these areas and the newness of the joint venture concept, our administrative team concluded that it would be better to form three separate joint ventures, so as to give us the opportunity to select those firms which were really the best.

Results

The problem St. Joseph faced was the development of a strategic plan for diversification without the benefit of market data, for businesses in which we had no experience and in a marketplace that was very competitive and constantly changing. The management actions we took consisted of a step-by-step process through which we developed that plan. In one sense, the strategic plan was the result we sought to achieve; in another sense, the end result will be the success or failure of that plan in the marketplace. It is too early to comment on the latter, but some additional comments can be made on the relative success of the developmental process of the plan. This success can be measured against three criteria:

1)   Did the plan stand the test of negotiations with those far more experienced in the home care markets?

2)   Was the plan flexible enough to permit modification without weakening its basic premises?

3)   Was the plan accepted internally?

Following the development of the plan, we commenced the selection process and began meeting with firms from each of the three types of home care businesses. Quite naturally, each firm had its own agenda and its preferred way of forming a joint venture. These meetings were a time of give and take, during which the plan's provisions and assumptions were severely tested. The plan withstood these tests, however, as the firms we approached confirmed our approach to diversification and even conceded that our plan was among the best organized and best thought-out they had seen. In addition, even weighing the worst-case scenario, we found promising opportunities in each of the businesses. Finally, the enthusiasm generated by both our plan and our organization confirmed (in our minds) our Hospital's competitive position.

As we proceeded through negotiations, we had a chance to refine the ideas and approaches in the proposals we received. For example, we decided on a limited fee-for-service arrangement in the "high-tech" business, which required no capital and little time. With routine home care, our revisions were just the opposite, as we determined that we needed to set up a new corporation for licensing purposes; this new corporation would then contract for day-to-day management. With DME, we contemplated setting up our own business, but finally returned to the original contractual joint venture called for in the plan. Setting up the three businesses in this manner created a good mix of capital and time requirements and the plan proved flexible enough to accommodate these changes.

Finally, the strategic plan was accepted internally. As we concluded negotiations, our team became more and more convinced that we were moving in the right direction. We came to feel comfortable with the plan we developed, as did those around us. This is not to say that implementation will be easy; but at least we have a blueprint which is easily understood, and which everyone had a part in developing.

Establishment of a Home Care Department Through Collaborative Efforts with a Sister Hospital

Organization Information

Providence Hospital was established in 1904 as the first general hospital in this metropolitan area. From its beginning, it has grown to a 260 bed general, acute care non-profit teaching organization including a 185 bed medical/surgical facility located in the older central section of the city, and a 75 bed psychiatric and substance abuse facility located in the rapidly growing southern suburbs. Providence offers a broad range of services including cardiac catheterization, angioplasty, and open heart surgery. It has approximately 500 full-time employees and a medical staff of 220 physicians and health professional affiliates representing virtually all specialties within the medical profession.

Providence Hospital is sponsored and operated under the auspices of a religious community of Sisters who oversee 40 health care facilities throughout the United States. It is a tax-exempt corporation with a nine-member board of trustees responsible for day-to-day operations. A regional corporation sponsored by the religious community serves as the corporate member of the hospital and retains certain reserve powers for non-routine matters.

Providence is located in the central portion of the state along a major interstate highway which connects the state's major population centers. The city has experienced moderate population growth in recent years, and now has a population of 100,000 .

Gist of the Problem

As Providence Hospital prepared to enter the home care market, it found itself faced with a number of challenges, including organizational approach and the responsibilities of and relationship between the concerned parties. Among the optional approaches was one that involved a collaborative effort with a sister hospital 100 miles away in a metropolitan area.

Description of the Problem

While Providence was preparing for the transition to the new Medicare Prospective Payment System, administrative discussions focused on the desirability of a home care program. However, no formal efforts had been initiated to evaluate and make recommendations regarding the establishment of such a program.

73

The vice president responsible for the nursing service division was assigned the task of assessing the need for home care services in the community. This assignment included identification of the objectives of a home care program, consideration of various organizational approaches, and the formulation of a specific recommendation and implementation plan. Periodic progress reports were provided to an administrator, who gave overall guidance for the project. In addition, progress reports were provided to the Administrative Council to assure collective ownership and support of the final recommendations.

Initially, the overall objectives of a home care program included:

1) the reduction of inpatient length of stay and provision of continuity of patient care following discharge;

2) extension of hospital services to the home setting, including, as appropriate, hyperalimentation, chemotherapy, parenteral and enteral nutritional therapies plus new products and technologies;

3) provision of private duty nursing, homemaker services, durable medical equipment and supplies for patients served through the program;

4) provision of an alternative to hospitalization and re-institutionalization by promoting family-centered health care and health education, especially for the elderly and those with chronic illness;

5) expansion of the hospital's revenue base and increase of market share.

After careful discussion, two basic organizational approaches were considered. The first centered on the in-house development of a home care department; the second involved contracting with an existing agency. With respect to the latter, proposals from three local home care agencies were solicited.

The project was discussed with representatives of the home care department at a sister hospital located in a major metropolitan area 100 miles to the south; the potential for a collaborative effort was explored and included in the evaluation. This sister hospital, acquired a few years ago by the same religious association that sponsors Providence Hospital, is a 129 bed facility located in an inner city area. Historically, it had experienced poor inpatient utilization, but has developed a comprehensive array of home health services. These services are not only provided to patients of the hospital but also by contract to another much larger tertiary care hospital sponsored by the same religious order.

While discussions regarding home health assistance to Providence were going forward, the sister hospital was considering incorporating the home care program with the intention of expanding into other markets. These markets included communities not served by the religious order, as well as those where it operated hospitals without home care programs.

As mentioned, Providence Hospital had identified a contractual relationship with an existing agency as one alternative; the potential for development of a joint program which would be operated as a subunit of the sister hospital's program evolved during discussion of this option. It was generally agreed that continuity of care would be enhanced by the hospital offering home health services directly; such care was viewed by the staff as a logical extension of the hospital's services. In addition, the only other acute care hospital in the community had recently initiated a home health program, and it was essential to offer the physicians practicing within the study hospital a comparable level of services because of the increasingly competitive nature of the market.

Proposals were solicited from three local home care agencies as well as from the sister hospital, and the potential for establishing a home care program directly operated by the hospital was assessed. The following advantages and disadvantages were identified:

1) Establish own department

   Advantages:
   a) exclusive control of hospital
   b) maximum revenue potential
   c) maintenance of philosophy of care

   Disadvantages:
   a) maximum hospital involvement in start-up and day-to-day management
   b) financial risk and start-up expenses borne by hospital
   c) time required to obtain licensure and certification may be considerable
   d) management expertise must be recruited

2) Contract with existing agency

   Advantages:
   a) time required to establish program reduced
   b) management expertise exists
   c) need for licensure/certification is eliminated
   d) hospital involvement in day-to-day management is minimized
   e) financial risk and start-up expenses borne by agency

   Disadvantages:
   a) loss of control of operations
   b) reduction of revenue potential

c) potential for compromising hospital's philosophy of care

d) potential for conflicting priorities between hospital and agency

Administrative Decision

After analyzing the advantages and disadvantages of the two major alternatives, members of the group agreed that a cooperative venture with the sister hospital could result in realizing the benefits of both alternatives while incurring few of the disadvantages. In addition, the group recognized that pursuit of this option would provide an opportunity to achieve the system-wide objectives of extending the mission of the sponsoring body and sharing services and resources already existing within the system.

Moreover, a cooperative program with the sister hospital would be consistent with the separate incorporation of the program to serve additional markets. It would reduce the financial risk, maximize the financial return, assure control by the sponsoring body, provide for a common philosophy of care, and reduce potential for conflicting priorities between the hospital and the agency. It was anticipated, however, that establishment of such a program would entail some logistical difficulties.

Based on a common view that a cooperative venture was clearly the preferred option, an agreement was reached and ultimately approved by the boards of trustees of both hospitals as well as by the regional corporate board. The essential elements of this agreement were as follows:

1) The program would be a subunit of the home care department of the sister hospital but would be allowed to utilize Providence Hospital's name in marketing the program.

2) The subunit would be provided with office space, utilities, parking, and housekeeping services in return for a percentage of the gross revenues, to a maximum annual amount.

3) The subunit would employ all personnel and provide both workers' compensation and general liability insurance.

4) The subunit would have responsibility for complying with the requirements of all statutes, laws, regulations and accrediting agencies having jurisdiction over the agency.

5) The subunit would assume full financial responsibility for start-up costs, operational expenses, and losses due to disallowed costs of service.

6) The subunit would agree to provide a full scope of services including as appropriate:

a) skilled nursing care
b) home health aide services
c) social services
d) physical therapy
e) speech therapy
f) medical/surgical supplies
g) equipment
h) other services as mutually agreed upon

7) The hospital would agree to help promote the agency and provide a Professional Advisory Board, including hospital staff and physicians.

8) The hospital would agree to purchase supplies and services for the agency where a cost saving benefit would be realized, and to submit a monthly itemized statement to the agency.

9) The hospital would retain authority to review and approve an overall annual business marketing plan for the program.

Following approval of the concepts and required agreements, the program was established and became operational.

Results

During the initial ten month period following establishment of the program, a total of 155 admissions and 2380 patient visits were recorded. Gross revenues totalled $121,911 with net revenues of $109,720. Total operational expenses were $115,948 during the same period. Included in these operational expenses was Providence's percentage share of gross revenues, in the amount of $8229 for the space provided.

Overall, the program is considered highly successful, and has been well-received by the employees, physicians, patients, and community. Among the factors contributing to this success are:

1) the existence of capable and experienced staff and proven programs;

2) the effective integration of the new program into existing hospital operations;

3) the utilization of a Professional Advisory Board to provide input and generate physician awareness of and support for the program;

4) the appointment of a respected medical director selected from the community to serve as a consultant to the agency;

5) utilization of and coordination with many other community agencies for services required by the patient;

6) discharge planning utilizing a multidisciplinary team approach to meet specific patient needs;

7) presentations by the director of the program to the medical staff;

8) periodic, concise news bulletins sent to the medical staff regarding program activities.

From a system-wide perspective, the overall objectives of extending the mission and sharing resources available within the system were realized. Several minor problems associated with the cooperative approach have appeared, however. They are the result of the dilution of administrative authority, the sharing of revenues, and the separate administrative processes within the two hospitals. Additionally, the administrative staff responsible for the main program at the sister hospital is not personally knowledgeable of the local medical staff or political environment. Finally, minor logistical problems have been encountered because the administrative management of the program is located 100 miles away. Overall, however, the program has proven to be mutually beneficial and has been expanded to several other hospitals within the system.

C. The Expanded Mission

"The Development of an Adolescent Chemical Dependency Program" is an example of an alternative delivery system taking the form of an expanded health care mission. Of particular interest here is the source of the incentive--community and board of trustee interest. The author investigated the feasibility of the program by consulting with experts, selecting a psychosocial model for treatment and visiting half-way houses, freestanding facilities, and existing hospital-based chemical dependency programs. When the feasibility of the program is established, and the determination to go ahead with the hospital-based unit is made, the team embarks on the developmental phase. This aspect is notable for its contingency method of arriving at an appropriate facility size, patient mix, and use of space--tinkering that is understandable in view of the newness of the program. Among the lessons to be learned from the author's experience is that feasibility and planning phases often take far longer than anticipated. "In a conservative medical community, decisions of this nature must be made slowly, so as to maintain the confidence of the medical staff, board of trustees, administration, and the community at large."

"Establishing a Multi-Agency Hospice Coalition" presents a model for cooperation among competing health care organizations; it shows mistrust overcome by a common effort to serve one overriding expanded mission and benefit all concerned parties. Hospice care, a newly emerged segment of the extended mission of health care providers, is not a diversification activity designed to expand revenue base and strengthen market share. Even with Medicare reimbursement, it is chronically underfunded and heavily reliant on volunteered services. It is primarily a response to real need. Cooperation among the principal parties in this case begins with the mutual recognition of a need for a system that eliminates the fragmented hospice care currently being delivered. A task force that represents the four hospitals and the visiting health agency identifies problems and subsequently formulates a set of recommendations. The coalition surveys active hospices in the area and selects elements of each which contribute to the design of the new hospice-- a hybrid of home care and inpatient care that utilizes the existing structure of the visiting agency to handle management, clinical, clerical, and financial matters. Responsibility for financing, provision of services, and control is shared by the coalition members.

The remarkable success of this hospice venture is compared to a less successful hospice program where politics, inflexibility of members, and the decision to establish a freestanding hospice facility are cited as factors contributing to the disappointing outcome. In contrast, the successful program is seen as an exemplary case of cooperation in a diversification venture. "In the midst of a competitive atmosphere, this example of mutual support and compromise bears witness to benefits

79

which can be derived when hospitals and community agencies work together."

The Development of an Adolescent Chemical Dependency Program

Organization Information

A multi-hospital organization has as its main facility a 500 bed teaching institution, Bretton Hospital. It is located on the fringe of a major metropolitan city that is currently experiencing urban decay. The short-stay acute care facility consists of 28 obstetrical beds, 30 pediatric beds, 45 psychiatric beds, with the balance for medical/surgical patients. Other facilities in the organization include four medical office buildings and a freestanding emergency room located 15 miles from the main facility.

Since its founding, the primary mission of this corporation has been to provide quality health care regardless of ability to pay; to provide a teaching atmosphere for all types of health personnel; and finally, to promote research. In the words of the hospital's biggest benefactor, the purpose of this eleemosynary organization is to "run a first-class hospital."

In the immediate geographic area of Bretton, there are three other major hospitals and several smaller ones. One of the three larger is a world renowned clinic with 1000 beds. The others include a university-operated institution with 950 beds, and a religious hospital of 500 beds. There is also an HMO that is growing at a 10-15 percent rate per year.

Gist of the Problem

There was no local inpatient treatment for chemical dependency available to adolescents in this large metropolitan area. Beginning in 1980, Bretton Hospital began to receive letters of support from influential persons in the community expressing interest in an adolescent chemical dependency program, and there was a similar interest among members of the board of trustees. Adolescent chemical dependency programs had been successful in other states primarily because state legislators had mandated insurance coverage through their state departments of insurance. Unfortunately no one on the administrative staff of Bretton Hospital possessed expertise in the development of a program of this nature. Moreover, relatively few meaningful statistics were available concerning the population required to support a rehabilitative program of this nature.

Description of the Problem

Bretton's CEO and the chairman of the board of trustees received unsolicited letters urging the hospital to initiate a program for adolescents harmfully involved with alcohol and drugs. Many of these letters were from community leaders and an even larger number were from school officials, teachers, and parents of children afflicted with one or more harmful addictive substances; others were from members of the clergy, as well as Bretton's own board of trustees. The number of letters increased, and as members of the board of trustees joined the campaign, it became apparent that careful investigation had to be undertaken.

As previously stated, no one on the administrative staff had experience with a program of this nature, and no staff physician had training in the treatment of adolescents suffering from chemical addiction. The casewriter was aware of the problems associated with many of the inner-city adult treatment programs, which added to our concerns regarding the establishment of an adolescent chemical dependency program at Bretton.

Administrative Decision

First, we had to decide who on the administrative staff should have direct responsibility for investigation of the program. It was decided that the author, who was the executive vice president and chief operating officer, and the newly appointed vice president for ambulatory services should be co-investigators of existing programs and should report back to the executive management team. The author was charged with the responsibility of preparing a recommendation for the executive team and board of trustees regarding the feasibility of the program. A second administrative problem was the need for medical input, a matter complicated by the question of whether chemical dependency treatment falls within the purview of medicine or mental health. Medical direction was to be provided by the director of pediatrics.

With the investigation team in place, several other administrative decisions had to be addressed. Expertise in adolescent chemical dependency was desperately needed, but consultants in this field were few and usually partial to a selected modality of treatment. Following several telephone conferences regarding existing programs, the author decided to engage a consulting firm in Minneapolis, which utilized what has been called the "Minnesota Model of Treatment." This modality of treatment is psychosocial in nature and follows the tenets of Alcoholics Anonymous, with minimal involvement of physicians and mental health workers. The decision was based on information provided by the successful treatment program regarding recidivism rates, longevity of abstinence, and perceptions of their effectiveness within the community. While personnel in the various programs felt their treatments were an asset to the community, research and statistical analysis showed that the Minnesota Model was indeed the most effective in the care and treatment of chemically dependent adolescents.

The investigation team concurred on using the Minnesota Model. It next decided which of the many existing programs to visit, and what criteria to use in the evaluation. The decision of which hospital units to visit was facilitated by the concentration of institutions in the Minneapolis area which utilized the Minnesota Model. Since it is known that adolescent chemical abuse programs consume very few hospital services after the initial medical evaluation (thus not supporting a hospital's large investment in ancillary services), the author decided to visit several halfway houses in order to measure them against the hospital-based and freestanding programs. The development of criteria for the evaluation phase (recidivism and abstinence rates) was much more difficult.

Before departing for Minneapolis, our team investigated freestanding programs in the local area. This part of the investigation phase proved to be very time-consuming and of little benefit. Most of the facilities (freestanding psychiatric hospitals, institutions known for the treatment of emotionally disturbed children, and a freestanding children's hospital) had no interest in a joint venture, or had philosophical disagreements with the treatment modality which had been selected. After several months of discussion, it was determined that our institution would have to do the program alone, within the hospital or another facility (which would have to be purchased or built). Concurrently the casewriter sought advice from the regional council on alcoholism. This proved to be an invaluable resource for statistical information.

A final administrative problem applied to the control of patient mix. The demographics of the area gave reason to suspect that a program of this nature would become the "dumping ground" for area teenagers who were perceived to be addicted to some form of chemical. Since this program would have to break even to be approved for implementation, we made a decision to eliminate emergency admissions and to limit indigent or no-pay admissions.

The author and the vice president for ambulatory care made a trip to Minnesota to review three hospital-based adolescent chemical dependency programs. We also planned to visit three halfway houses, as well as certain consultants who were trained in and practiced the Minnesota Model of treatment. During visits to halfway houses, we tried to discern the staff's attitude toward hospital-based programs and freestanding programs. In these discussions, we found that most staff members favored the hospital programs because of the available personnel and the low ratio of clients to trained chemical-dependency counselors. Further, the halfway house personnel suggested that the image of a hospital seemed to attract those chemically-dependent persons who were more serious about sobriety.

Except for the remarks from the halfway house personnel, little evidence had been offered to support an in-hospital program. The author's primary concerns were (1) the cost of a hospital bed as opposed to the cost of a less sophisticated setting; (2) the lack of use of hospital ancillary services; (3) the need for recreational facilities; and (4) a program design that used few medical services. These concerns were shared with the entire administrative team, the consultants, and the medical director.

It was also known that the only alternative to using hospital facilities was to purchase an existing facility or to enter into a joint venture. Since the joint venture aspect had been reviewed earlier and found lacking, the remaining option was to buy a facility or build one. We recognized that the financial requirements of developing a separate facility would be too great and the required time too long. Consequently, the team decided to develop an in-hospital program.

Results

A certificate of need application for a 35 bed adolescent chemical dependency program was prepared and submitted to the state health department and the local planning authority with a request for expedited review. At the same time, a long and detailed letter from the regional council on alcoholism was submitted to both authorities, demonstrating community support of the program. The application was deemed complete with only a few minor questions from the state department of health, but the request for an expedited review was denied. Despite a few letters which did not favor the program (submitted by existing adult treatment centers which also accepted adolescents), the certificate of need was approved.

Having gained approval, we began to remodel an existing nursing unit. In addition to preparing the unit, the author hired a director for the program who had experience at another hospital program, and who was a recovered alcoholic and former drug abuser himself. This individual had had extensive training as a drug abuse counselor, and had obtained an undergraduate management degree. The hiring of the director early in the construction phase allowed him almost four months to establish community contacts, set policies and procedures, and generate his network of referrals.

Additionally, the new director had dealt with the question of controlling payor mix and had established a routine for admissions which would screen out those persons unable to pay for the services. One bed was set aside to serve indigent patients who exhibited a willingness to complete the program.

Although the certificate of need was approved for 35 beds, the initial unit was sized to seven beds for the evaluation period and 14 beds for primary treatment. The evaluation phase consisted of an intensive five to seven day assessment program within a locked unit. This was followed by four weeks of primary treatment in which the patient received individual and group counseling, and participated in required reading, lectures, occupational therapy, and remedial or continuing education. The author made the decision to limit the size of the unit to 21 beds, because of space restrictions, remodeling costs, and other advantages associated with beginning a program on a small scale.

The facility opened with three patients in the evaluation unit, and after a week of operation, the seven bed unit was filled. After the first three weeks of operation, the entire unit was filled and a waiting list was started. A long waiting list concerned us, as it could discourage referral sources and shift allegiance to other facilities. Since it was also obvious that we were unable to provide enough beds to serve the apparent need, an expedient resolution of the problem was required.

The unit had been built with oversized rooms, out of consideration for the length of stay and the greater need of adolescents to move around. We decided to convert all of the semi-private rooms on the primary care unit into three-bed units, and to leave the evaluation unit alone. Shortly after its opening, some young clients in the program decided to break out of the facility for an evening binge. Of the five persons who took part in this activity, four were immediately dismissed from the program and the fifth was put on probationary status. Not only did this event help to alleviate the pressure on the waiting list, but it also pointed out a need to tighten up the admission criteria and the evaluation period.

The unit operated at an occupancy rate in excess of 100 percent for nine of the eleven months it was in operation in its first year. The project was so successful that plans were developed to expand the unit to 28 beds on a permanent basis by remodeling adjacent space.

Although the author initially had a great deal of apprehension concerning the development of an in-house adolescent chemical dependency program, the project was extremely successful and profitable for the institution. Unfortunately, it required a long planning period. In a conservative medical community, decisions of this nature must be made slowly so as to maintain the confidence of the medical staff, board of trustees, administration, and the community at large. This is true especially when converting general short term medical and surgical beds to a non-traditional, though apparently very much needed, use.

Organization Information

Woodcourt Hospital is a 250 bed general, voluntary non-profit institution governed by a board of trustees. The facility has been in operation for 28 years; it services 12 suburban towns and boroughs in an area with approximately 210,000 people. Three other area hospitals are a 560 bed Catholic teaching institution, a 250 bed general hospital, and a similar 215 bed general facility; all three are voluntary non-profit institutions governed by boards of trustees. The populations served and years of service vary from institution to institution, but all have been in operation longer than Woodcourt Hospital. The fifth health care provider is a visiting health agency with roughly 60 employees serving over 80,000 visits per year on a total budget of $2 million.

Gist of the Problem

Despite a growing national demand for hospice services, funding to support such programs is generally less than is required. Individually, hospitals are developing inpatient hospice units to take advantage of reimbursement for acute inpatient care, but this practice tends to fragment hospice care and deviates from a basic hospice principle of permitting the patient to die with dignity in their home. A Task Force representing the four hospitals and visiting health agency was organized to develop and implement an innovative coalition which (1) takes maximum advantage of available home care and hospital reimbursement; (2) creates additional financial support through hospital subsidization; and (3) avoids further fragmentation of hospice services in the region.

Description of the Problem

The problems facing hospice care in the early 1980s were both regional and national in scope. In the mid and late 1970s hospice programs generated a great deal of interest and support throughout the country; a federally funded national pilot program involving 26 hospices had improved the provision of services, but there was no way such a program could meet the growing demands for providing care to the terminally ill. Many hospitals began to develop their own support programs, either through the formation of inpatient units or by sponsoring multidisciplinary support teams to assist the patients and families. As the demand for hospice care grew, however, hospitals reached the limits of funding they could reasonably provide to such programs, and a severe strain was placed on many of the voluntary services which were so essential to hospice success. The provision of inpatient hospice care was rarely coordinated with home care agencies and this tended to fragment hospice services and break up the continuity of care so important to the patient's support.

Reimbursement was available for acute care in hospitals, of course, and for routine home care, but the amount of coverage varied widely depending on the age of the patient and the type of insurance carried. Even with extensive coverage, many essential hospice services, such as palliative and respite care, bereavement counseling, and terminal care were either denied outright to patients or were subject to challenge by third party payors. In addition, because hospice services frequently involve substantial investments of time and expense, the reimbursement provided by existing coverages was frequently insufficient to cover the full cost of providing these services. Hospice programs routinely ran large operational deficits which they attempted to cover by donations and grants, or though subsidization by more profitable hospital acute care or home care services. More often than not, however, they failed in that effort.

One of the 26 hospices to receive federal funding was located in a freestanding facility west of Woodcourt Hospital, but outside its immediate service area. While this was a well-known and well-respected hospice, it too was undergoing financial and reorganizational problems, and within a year had to abandon its independent status and move into an underutilized nursing unit in an adjacent hospital. Woodcourt Hospital was a strong supporter of the hospice concept, and did everything it could through its social services department to assist this neighboring program. It was not long, however, before a neighboring and competitive institution announced its intention to form a hospice program, and it began to appear that hospice services would fragment completely in our region with no one institution or agency being able to fully support a program.

Representatives of the visiting health agency approached the four hospitals in its service area to talk about forming a hospice coalition. Because of the casewriter's administrative responsibility for social services and involvement in supporting the local hospice programs, he was asked to meet with these representatives to discuss the merits of this idea. The concept appeared simple: have the four hospitals and visiting health agency jointly form a hospice which would serve all the patients in the region and enable us to pool collective resources and avoid duplicating each other's efforts. The author was asked to represent Woodcourt in this effort.

A special Task Force consisting of representatives from each of the hospitals and the visiting health agency met to discuss whether it was feasible to pursue a joint coalition. These were competitive hospitals with a poor record of cooperation. Each hospital did have a common link to the visiting health agency, in that each appointed one representative to serve on that agency's board of trustees. But this was a weak basis on which to build a coalition.

The difficulties that confronted this Task Force were significant:

1) Hospice care had already begun to splinter, and at least two members of the Task Force had vested interests in their own programs.

2) Inpatient hospice units were then in vogue and there was a tendency to identify with them rather than with the home-based program being advocated by the visiting health agency.

3) Reimbursement for hospice programs was practically non-existent, grants were becoming scarce, donations provided insufficient operational support, and all of the hospitals faced a new and uncertain reimbursement methodology: DRGs.

4) Physician support for hospice programs varied significantly within the region; it was obvious that a major selling job would be necessary if a large-scale hospice program was to be successful.

As if these problems were not enough, each member of the Task Force recognized the uniqueness of the project: it had not been done before.

Administrative Decision

Within a few months, the Task Force had developed a cooperative spirit and reached a number of significant conclusions:

1) Establishing a whole new umbrella organization for the hospice program would be cumbersome, duplicative, and extremely expensive.

2) A better approach would be to utilize the existing organizational structure of the visiting health agency and provide guidance from the sponsoring members through an Advisory Committee.

3) The role of a medical director would be a key factor; the position should be rotated among the representative medical staffs.

4) Each sponsoring organization should contribute an equitable share toward underwriting the costs of the hospice program and providing services-in-kind.

With the strong support of each hospital's chief executive officer, our Task Force developed a program and a cooperative agreement which was subsequently endorsed and signed by all the participating organizations.

The first hurdle the Task Force had to overcome was the mutual suspicion which had developed over time. While the executive officers of the participating organizations were friendly and cooperative to a degree, institutional cooperation usually broke down at the departmental/operational level. Fortunately, all of the members of the Task Force had received a strong endorsement for a cooperative effort from the CEOs. In addition, the four hospitals were represented by relatively young assistant administrators who were not conditioned by past difficulties, who clearly understood the essential need for a joint hospice effort, and who embraced the cooperative spirit so essential to the group's success. The leader of the Task Force was selected from among the four.

A further factor contributing to the successful group dynamics was the role of the visiting health agency. While it had more expertise in hospice services and was better suited for the major role in the hospice program, the agency's representatives took a low-key approach and left much of the initial discussion and debate to the hospital representatives. It was also fully supportive of a cooperative effort even if that meant having its own control over the program diluted through a five-way coalition.

An additional factor which led to a cooperative spirit was the decision of the 215 bed hospital to relinquish control over its own hospice program and allow it to be incorporated into the cooperative effort. In truth, this hospital had little choice because (1) its program was not a great success on its own merits, (2) it was obvious that the other three hospitals were committed to proceed with or without its participation, and (3) the visiting health agency was committed to the joint effort and would have withdrawn its support from a single institution program. Nevertheless, their decision to relinquish control removed a major obstacle and certainly set the stage for further development of the program.

At the outset, the Task Force identified as its mission the development of a detailed report outlining the structure, services, benefits, and problems related to the establishment of a centralized hospice organization. Following a survey of active hospices in the area, the Task Force selected the best elements of each and combined these in a program description. While an inpatient unit was considered, it was deemed by all involved to be too expensive a proposition, lacking regular sources of reimbursement. This was evident from the experience of freestanding hospice units throughout the country. The Task Force endorsed the concept of a home care-oriented hospice program with back-up inpatient support provided by each of the hospitals. While we recognized that this would provide a less-than-ideal patient setting for the terminally ill, we believed that through inservice or even designated hospice areas, each of the hospitals could provide an acceptable inpatient environment, and we could thus avoid a costly freestanding inpatient unit.

Having determined the kind of program we wanted, the Task Force next proceeded to develop the organization and budgets necessary to operate it. At this point, our group dynamics and cooperative spirit worked against us, for we collectively put "blinders" on and thought only in terms of a new organization with a new board of directors. As the structure of this organization grew, so did its cost of operation, until ultimately we began to question whether we could even afford a cooperative effort. At this critical juncture, one of the Task Force members pointed out that we would be foolish to construct something which already existed. The obvious wisdom of this insight removed the group's blinders, and we recognized that by utilizing the organizational structure of the visiting health agency, we could accomplish the same ends without a cumbersome, duplicative and extremely expensive new organization.

The Task Force resolved to use the existing management, clinical, clerical, and financial staff of the visiting health agency to run the hospice. The agency, in turn, agreed to formalize the hospice services as a separate program within its organization, and requested financial support in two areas: (1) payments for a part-time medical director for the program, which would be essential for its success and which was not routinely part of a home health agency; and (2) subsidization to offset projected deficits resulting from the hospice operation. The Task Force agreed that each of the hospitals should share equally in the salary expense of the medical director who would be employed by the visiting health agency. In addition, the agency agreed to cover any hospice operating deficits from surpluses generated from its routine home care services, and the hospitals agreed to make up any difference should those surpluses not prove to be sufficient. This agreement removed some of the financial burden from the visiting health agency and provided them with greater peace of mind.

Collective control over the hospice program would be exercised through a specially appointed Advisory Committee which would be responsible for programmatic and financial review and for making recommendations to the Board of Trustees of the visiting health agency. Since the hospitals also appointed one member to this Board, they could exercise control over the hospice's operations at two levels. The hospitals also had additional leverage in the option to remove their financial support if they felt the hospice program was not responsive to the patients' or institution's needs.

With regard to services-in-kind, each hospital agreed to commit its public relations, volunteers, social services and nursing resources to making the program a success. Each hospital also agreed to provide space and supplies as necessary to underwrite the operating expenses. It was also understood that the Task Force representatives would become the operating core of the Advisory Committee.

Finally, the Task Force agreed to develop a medical advisory committee for the hospice program made up of interested physicians from each of the participating hospitals. In addition to providing guidance to the hospice, this group would also serve as liaison to the respective medical staffs and provide a mechanism for informing and educating area physicians about the services available. The salaried medical director would be chairman of this committee. In the interest of maintaining political neutrality, it was agreed that the medical director position be rotated on an annual basis among the four medical staffs involved. In this manner, a core of hospice "experts" could be developed over time within each hospital's medical staff.

Results

The results of the Task Force's efforts were remarkable. The program concept and cooperative agreement which was developed were readily accepted and endorsed by all the participants. The response of area physicians was very positive, and a tremendous amount of goodwill was generated among the coalition members. Meetings of public relations representatives from participating hospitals were held to develop an overall P. R. program. This was subsequently implemented; it received strong local support in each hospital's service area. The program also generated interest and enthusiasm among the physicians at each hospital.

Meetings were held with hospital representatives from nursing and social services to coordinate the provision of hospice services, arrange for inservice programs, and generate a means for channeling interested volunteers into the hospice volunteer program. The "grass roots" support which resulted from these meetings contributed significantly to the initial and ongoing success of the hospice. In addition, admitting processes and discharge planning were worked out to assure smooth transitions from inpatient to home care and vice versa. The direct lines of communication which were developed helped resolve many operational issues and generated a collective vested interest in the program's ultimate success. Each hospital also appointed a liaison to the hospice "team" so as to facilitate communication and smooth operations.

In the first six months of the coalition's hospice program, it admitted over 100 patients and generated an operating deficit of $14,000. In the following year, the number of patients admitted increased to 275 and the deficit increased to $28,000. During this same period, the program coordinated over 2700 volunteer hours of support for the patients and their families. Over the next two years, the number of patients grew at a modest rate to 318. Volunteer time grew at roughly 15% per year and reached over 3600 hours in the second year. In the same period, the operating deficit started to decline and dropped precipitously when Medicare introduced reimbursement for certified hospice services. After three years, the hospice program was at a break-even point financially and its overall budget had increased from an initial $226,000 to $771,000. It is worth noting that despite the deficits generated by the hospice services, the visiting health agency's other operating surpluses were always sufficient to cover them, and the hospitals were never asked to subsidize an operating deficit. In all respects, the hospice coalition has proven to be a highly successful model for implementing this program and has brought badly needed and high quality services to a large number of patients in the region.

Perhaps the best measure of the Task Force's success comes from a comparison of its results with those of another coalition with whom the author was concurrently involved. This second cooperative effort was in a different county and involved five hospitals, a visiting nurse association, and one of the 26 federally funded hospice programs. After being housed in an underutilized nursing unit for over a year, the hospice attempted to generate support for relocation to a different site.

On the surface, this coalition had all the elements and potential for success that existed with the Task Force. However, politics, a lack of true cooperative spirit, and an emphasis on inpatient care all contributed to a less successful effort. The hospice leadership insisted on maintaining independent control over the program, viewed the visiting nurse association as totally subservient to their directives, and took as the ultimate objective the establishment of a freestanding inpatient hospice facility. This unreasonable and inflexible attitude created ill-will among the participants and almost guaranteed that the program would encounter financial difficulties. The lack of cooperation led to limited growth and ultimately prevented the program from achieving significant success.

In contrast, the hospice coalition established by the Task Force continues to prosper, and the innovative model which was created has proven itself. Ultimately, this model fit in well with hospice regulations established by the federal government. In addition, the cooperation begun with the hospice coalition carried over into other projects such as the establishment of emergency medical systems. When hospitals and community agencies work together in an atmosphere of mutual support and compromise, considerable benefits for all may result.

Part Three: Bibliography

"Alternative Delivery Arena Evokes Melange of Approaches." Business and Health, 1:3 (January 1984), 29-34.

American Hospital Association. "Environmental Assessment: Overview 1987." Chicago, 1987.

American Medical Association. A Physician's Guide to Preferred Provider Organizations, Chicago, 1983.

Anderson, Odin, et al., HMO Development: Patterns and Prospects. University of Chicago: Pluribus Press, 1985.

Atkinson, Stanley, "Growth of HMOs Challenges Traditional Health Care." Health Progress, 68:3 (April 1987), 50-53.

Barger, S. Brian, et al., The PPO Handbook. Rockville, MD: Aspen Publication, 1984.

Boland, Peter, ed., The New Health care Market. Homewood, IL: Dow Jones-Irwin, 1985.

Boland, Peter, "Questioning Assumptions About Preferred Provider Arrangements." Inquiry, 22 (Summer 1985), 132-41.

Borchardt, Peter, and Thomas Davis, "Health Plan Networks:A New Delivery Option." Business and Health, (July 1987), 29-31.

Center for Health Administration Studies, "Selective Contracting: Proceedings of the Twenty-Seventh Annual George Bugbee Symposium on Hospital Affairs." University of Chicago: CHAS Publications, 1985.

Christianson, Jon, "The Impact of HMOs: Evidence and Research Issues." Journal of Health, Politics, Policy, and Law, 5:2 (Spring 1980), 354-67.

Christianson, Jon, and W. McClure, "Competition in the Delivery of Medical Care." New England Journal of Medicine, 301:15 (1979), 812-18.

Cowan, David, Preferred Provider Organizations, Rockville, MD: Aspen Publication, 1984.

Dalton, J.J., "HMOs and PPOs: Similarities and Differences." Health Care Finance, 13:3 (Spring 1987), 8-18.

de Lissovoy, Gregory, et al., "Preferred Provider Organizations: Today's Models and Tomorrow's Prospects." Inquiry, 23:1 (Spring 1986), 7-15.

Egdahl, Richard, "Managed Care Programs: Danger of Undercare." Hospitals, July 5, 1986, 136.

Ellenbogen, P.S., et al., "Alternative Delivery Systems: Do They Reduce the Aggregate Cost of Health Services?" NC Medical Journal, 48:9 (September 1986), 421-2.

Fein, Rashi, Medical Care, Medical Costs: The Search for a Health Insurance Policy, Cambridge: Harvard University Press, 1986.

Feldman, R., et al., "The Competitive Impact of Health Maintenance Organizations on Hospital Finances: An Exploratory Study." J Health Politics, Policy and Law, 10:4 (Winter 1986), 675-97.

Frank, Richard, and W.P. Welch, " The Competitive Effects of HMOs: A Review of the Evidence." Inquiry, 22:2 (Summer 1985), 148-61.

Ginsburg, Paul, and Glenn Hackbarth, "Alternative Delivery Systems and Medicare." Health Affairs, (Spring 1986), 6-22.

Ginsburg, Paul, et al., "Who Joins a PPO?" Business and Health, 4:2 (February 1987), 36-38.

Ginzberg, Eli, "The Destabilization of Health Care." New England Journal of Medicine, 315:12 (1986), 757-61.

Ginzberg, Eli, "The Delivery of Health Care: What Lies Ahead ?" Inquiry, 20:3 (Fall 1983), 201-17.

Ginzberg, Eli, "The Restructuring of U.S. Health Care." Inquiry, 22:3 (Fall 1985), 272-81.

Ginzberg, Eli, ed.The U.S. Health Care System. Totowa, NJ: Rowman and Allanheld, 1985.

Ginzberg, Eli, "A Hard Look At Cost Containment." New England Journal of Medicine, 316:18 (April 30, 1987), 1151-54.

Goldfield, Norbert, and Seth Goldsmith, eds., Alternative Delivery Systems, Rockville, MD: Aspen Publisher, 1987.

Goldsmith, Jeff, Can Hospitals Survive? The New Competitive Health Care Market, Homewood, IL: Dow Jones-Irwin, 1981.

Henderson, John, "Health Maintenance Organizations--Industry Structure and Trends." Health Industry Today, (October 1986), 54-63.

Hunt, Michie, "Managed Care in the 1990s." Health Care Strategic Management, 3:12 (December 1985), 20-24.

Inquiry, 23:3 (Fall 1986).

Kendrick, Martha, "PPOs: A Challenge to HMOs." The Group Health Journal, 6:2 (Fall 1985), 22-27.

Kress, John, and James Singer, HMO Handbook, Rockville, MD: Aspen Systems Corporation, 1975.

Luft, Harold, Health Maintenance Organizations: Dimensions of Performance, New York: John Wiley and Sons, 1981.

Luft, Harold, "How Do Health Maintenance Organizations Achieve Their Savings?" New England Journal of Medicine, 298:24 (1978), 1336-42.

Rahn, Gary, ed., Hospital-Sponsored Health Maintenance Organizations: Issues for Decision Makers, Chicago: American Hospital Publishing, 1987.

Richman, Daniel, "Number of PPOs Rises at Fast Pace." Modern Healthcare, 16:2 (June 6, 1986), 138-40.

Shouldice, Robert, "Negotiating with Alternative Delivery Systems." Medical Group Management Review, (January 1987), 9-11.

Tibbitts, Samuel, and Dennis Strum, The New Healthcare Market, Homewood, IL: Dow Jones-Irwin, 1985, 934-46.

Trauner, Joan, and Sandra Hunt, "Hospitals that Contract with PPOs: Who Are They?" Business and Health, 3:4 (March 1986), 30-33.

Wolinsky, Frederic, "The Performance of Health Maintenance Organizations: An Analytic Review." Milbank Memorial Fund Quarterly, 58:4 (1980), 537-87.